PUBLIC LIBRARY PLANS FOR THE BOOK COLLECTION

ISBN 978-157440-354-1   ©2015 Primary Research Group Inc.

Table of Contents

Public Library Plans for the Book Collection

3

THE QUESTIONNAIRE

Introductory Information

1. Please give us the following contact information

    A. Name:
    B. Organization:
    C. Title:
    D. Country:
    E. Email Address:

2. What is the approximate size of your library's service area?

3. What is the size of your full time equivalent library staff?

Alternatives to Print

4. How comfortable would you say your library is with the substitution of eBooks for print books? When does the acquisition of an eBook title lead you to eliminate or reduce your holdings of the print version of the same title?

5. What was your library's spending on print books in each of the following years?

    A. 2014
    B. 2015
    C. 2016 (anticipated)

6. How much did your library spend on eBooks in each of the following years?

    A. 2014
    B. 2015
    C. 2016 (anticipated)

7. What was your library's spending on print children's books in each of the following years?

    A. 2014
    B. 2015
    C. 2016 (anticipated)

8. What was your library's spending on eBooks intended primarily for children in each of the following years:

    A. 2014
    B. 2015
    C. 2016 (anticipated)

Predictive Models for Print Book Use

9. What factors does the library take into account when it makes print book culling decisions?

Collection Volume

10. What is the total number of volumes in your library's print book collection for each of the following years:

    A. 2014
    B. 2015
    C. 2016 (anticipated)

11. In which areas has the library been most aggressive in eliminating print titles and why in these areas?

12. What has happened to your library's print book collection over the past five years? Is it larger than it was five years ago, in what areas has it grown? If it is smaller, in what areas has it diminished?

13. In your view what will happen to your library's print book collection over the next five years? Will it become larger or smaller? If so, what areas will be most affected and why? Will spending remain the same? Increase or decrease?

Print Book Culling Strategy

14. Approximately what percentage of your print book collection did you cull in the past year?

15. If the library has changed its book acquisitions and/or book collection culling strategy over the past five years, or expects to change it soon, please describe these changes.

16. In what areas do you believe that the library will be most aggressive in culling print books in the future? In what areas or subjects do you believe that the library is likely to increase spending on print books?

Space Issues

17. If the library has reduced the size of its book collection in recent years, has this led to an increase in space that the library can use for other purposes?

   A. Yes
   B. No

18. If space has been freed-up over the past five years how much space and how is this space now being deployed?

Opinion of Library Patrons

19. Has the library surveyed its patrons on their preferences for print vs. digital resources as a prelude to decision making on reducing the size of book collections?

   A. Yes
   B. No

20. Which phrase would you say best describes your Friends of the Library organization about using library resources for increasing spending on print books or eBooks

   A. Tend to be more supportive of eBooks
   B. Tend to be more supportive of Print Books
   C. Don't really take a position on the issue

21. In your view local school districts in the library's service area tend to want the library to:

   A. Prioritize eBooks in library purchasing decisions
   B. Prioritize Print Books in library purchasing decisions
   C. Don't seem to have a preference
   D. Impact on Use of Storage Space

22. Does the library use offsite storage for books, journals and other printed materials?

   A. Yes
   B. No

23. Has the amount of space used for offsite storage increased or decreased in recent years and if so by how much? Also what has been the trend in storage costs?

24. What kinds of data does your library use in making print materials culling decisions and how does each data set contribute to your decision making?

25. Approximately what percentage of your culled book collection is given away to schools, libraries, charitable agencies or other venues?

26. Mention some incidents, if any, in which the library was forced to back track and restore access to print copies of materials that had been culled in printed form.

Support for Print or Digital

27. Are particular types of library users more likely to prefer print and lobby the library for more spending on print books? If so who?

28. How is print collection culling at your library organized? Which librarians are involved in the decision-making? Who makes the final decisions in particular areas? Who reviews decisions? Who overturns decisions?

29. What is the greatest mistake that the library has made in its print book collection development decision making in recent years?

30. What advice do you have for your peers on planning for the future in public library book purchasing?

PARTICIPANTS' LIST

Alexander Memorial Library
Alexandria Public Library
Barrett Memorial Library
Brazoria County Library System
Brillion Public Library
Calmar Public Library
City of Onalaska Public Library
Clarks Public Library
Cockrell Hill Public Library
Cold Lake Public Library
Cooke County Library
Crockett County Public Library
Douglas County Libraries
Drumright Public Library
Dyer Library
Edwards Public Library
Edythe Dyer Community Library
Erie City Public Library
Fairfield Library Association, Inc.
Fairfield Public Library
Falls City Public Library
Garnavillo Public Library
Goliad County Library
Hemphill County Library
High River Library
Hondo Public Library
Indian Valley Public Library
Katahdin Public Library
Kennedy Public Library
Keya Paha County Library
Keytesville Library
Krum Public Library
Laramie County Library System
Larsen Family Public Library
Lehi City Public Library
Marcus Public Library
Mattoon Public Library

Melcher-Dallas Public Library
Memphis Public Library
Menlo Public Library
Monticello Public Library
New Braunfels Public Library
New Waverly Public Library
Newkirk Public Library
Norelius Community Library
Ohio Genealogical Society
Olds Municipal Library
Paulding County Carnegie Library
Pincher Creek & District Municipal Library
Post Public Library
Pueblo City-County Library District
Rockford Carnegie Library
Southlake Public Library
Sulphur Springs Public Library
Thorhild Library
Tipp City Public Library
Vista Grande Public Library
Washburn Memorial Library
Waskom Public Library
Will Rogers Library
Yellowhead County Library Board

Characteristics of the Sample

The approximate population of library service area:

Service Area Population	#
Less than 3000	16
3000+ -7000	15
7000-19000	15
More than 19000	16
Total	62

The size of full time equivalent library staff:

FTE Library Staff Size	#
1 or less	19
1+ -2.8	13
2.8+ -6	14
More than 6	16
Total	62

Library's spending on print books:

Spending on Print Books $	#
Less than 4500	16
4500-14000	16
14000-30000	15
More than 30000	15
Total	62

SUMMARY OF MAIN FINDINGS

INTRODUCTORY INFORMATION

Characteristics of the Sample

Sixty-two public libraries participated in the Survey of Public Library Plans. For the Print Book Collection. We broke the sample out by three subcategories: service-area population, number of full time equivalent staff and spending on print books. First, we asked the participants to identify their libraries approximate service area. Of the sixty-two libraries, sixteen serve a population of less than 3,000, fifteen serve 3,000-7,000, fifteen serve 7,000-19,000 and sixteen have a service population of more than 19,000. Next we asked how many full time equivalent staff the libraries employ. Nineteen of the sixty-two libraries have 1 or fewer full time equivalent staff members, thirteen have 1+-2.8, fourteen have 2.8-6, and sixteen have more than 6. Finally, we asked the participants to identify their library's spending on print books. Of the entire sample, sixteen spend less than $4,500, sixteen spend $4,500-$14,000, fifteen spend $14,000-$30,000 and fifteen spend more than $30,000 on print books.

ALTERNATIVES TO PRINT

Substituting eBooks for Print Books

We asked the participants how comfortable they would say their library is with the substitution of eBooks for print books. We also asked them when the acquisition of an eBook title would lead to the elimination of or reduction of holdings of the print version of the same title. We received sixty responses to this open-ended question.

Participants were fairly evenly divided in their responses, in terms of a negative or positive reaction to the inclusion of eBooks in their library collections. Many libraries do not yet offer eBooks and some said they were very uncomfortable with the idea of eBooks replacing print books in their collection. As one participant said, "The library is not comfortable with eBooks. I would not eliminate a print book just because I had it as an eBook." On the other hand, a great number are very comfortable with the decision to offer an eBook in place of a print book. One participant told us, "Our library is completely comfortable with the interchangeability of print and digital. We often reduce the number of copies of a title we will acquire if we have unlimited access to the same title in digital."

Public Library Plans for the Book Collection

The trend is overwhelmingly towards building and supplementing a collection with eBooks but not yet as a substitute for print titles. "We purchase eBooks as an additional format, not to replace existing" was a sentiment expressed over and over again. While eBooks are increasing in popularity with the libraries very few of the survey participants said they were comfortable with eBooks replacing print copies in their collections.

EBook Spending in 2014

We asked the participants to identify how much their library spent on eBooks in 2014 (all figures in $ US). Of the entire sample, the mean was $10,499.97 and the mean was $650 in a range of $0 to $273,000. Across all subgroups, mean spending increased with the size of the service area, size of full time equivalent staff, and as print book spending increased.

Broken out by library service area population, libraries serving a population of less than 3,000 spent the least on eBooks in 2014, a mean of $120 and a median of $0 in a range of $0-$500 while libraries serving more than 19,000 spent the most, a mean of $37,119.19 and a median of $8,250 in a range of $0-$273,000. In the middle of the group, libraries with a service area population between 3,000 and 7,000 spent a mean $896.20 and those serving 7,000-9,000 spent a mean $2,089.87 on eBooks in 2014.

EBook Spending in 2015

We then asked the participants to identify how much their library had spent on eBooks in 2015. There was an overall increase in eBook spending from the year prior. Of the entire sample, the mean was $12,949.33 and the median was $1,000 in a range of $0-$275,000. Once more, spending increased as service population, staff, and print book spending increased. The annual increase in spending on eBooks was 23.3%.

Again, the results were broken out by the population of the libraries' service areas. Libraries with a service area population of less than 3,000 once again reported a range of $0-$500 and a median of $0 but their mean spending increased to $170, up $50 from the previous year. Libraries serving a population of 3,000-7,000 saw their mean and median spending increase to $1,006.80 and $500 respectively. Libraries with a service area population of 7,000-19,000 saw no changes to their mean and median spending on eBooks between the two years but their range dropped from $0-$10,000 in 2014 to $0-$8,000 in 2015. Finally, libraries with a service area population of more than 19,000 saw significant increases in their eBook spending in 2015. Their mean spending was $46,307.63 and their median was $15,500 in a range $0-$275,000.

EBook Spending in 2016

We concluded the series of questions on public library eBook spending by asking the participants how much they anticipate their library will spend on eBooks in 2016. Of the entire sample, the mean amount was $14,989.92 and the median was $1,200 in a range of $0-$300,000. The annual rate of spending increase in 2016 is expected to be 15.75%.

Broken out across all subcategories, none of the library groups anticipate spending less on eBooks in 2016 than they did in 2015. Overall, libraries with a service area population of less than 3,000 plan on spending the least on eBooks in 2016, a mean of just $203.33 and median of $0 in a range of $0-$1,000. The libraries that plan on spending the most are those that spend the most on print books, over $30,000. Their projected mean spending on eBooks in 2016 is $55,113.33 and their median is $20,000. These libraries reported a range of $1,200 to $30,000 as did libraries with more than 6 full time equivalent staff members. Libraries with a service area population of more than 19,000 were the only other group to not report a minimum of $0; their minimum was $500.

CHILDREN'S BOOKS

Print Children's Books Spending in 2014

The next series of questions focused on public library spending on print children's books. We began by asking, "What was your library's spending on print children's books in 2014?" Of the entire sample, the mean was $22,803.28 and the median was $4,645.50 in a range of $0-$512,500, considerably higher than the highest figures projected for spending on all eBooks. The libraries' mean spending on children's books in print format increased as service population, staff size, and overall spending on print books increased.

The results were broken out by the population of the libraries' service areas. Libraries serving less than 3,000 spent a mean $1,902.81 on printed children's books in 2014, this figure rose to $3,263.64 for those serving 3,000-7,000, and then the amount more than doubled to $6,766.47 for those with a service area population of 7,000-19,000. Libraries with a service area population of more than 19,000 spent a substantial mean $77,056.69 on print children's books. Their median figure was $17,203.50 with a minimum of $2,000 and a maximum of $512,500.

The results were further broken out by the libraries' level of overall spending on all print books. Libraries that spend less than $4,500 on print books spent a mean $1,412.19 and a median $925 in a range of $0-$9,000 on print children's books in 2014. For libraries with print book spending between $4,500 and $14,000 the mean spending on printed children's books was $3,314.44 and the median was $3,775 in a range of just $0-$8,000. For libraries that spend between $14,000 and $30,000 the mean and median figures were $6,910 and $8,000 in a range of $2,000-$12,407. Finally, libraries that spend more than $30,000 on print books spent a mean $82,301.84 and a median $22,000 on print children's books in 2014. Their reported range was $5,527.64-$512,500.

Public Library Plans for the Book Collection

Print Children's Books Spending in 2015

Next we asked the participants how much their libraries had spent on print children's books in 2015. Of the entire sample, the mean figure increased by a healthy 5.7% to $24,114.29 and the range also increased from the year prior to $0- $535,490.00. In contrast, the median figure dropped to $4,250.00. Libraries that spend between $4,500 and $14,000 on print books, those that have 1-2.8 time equivalent staff members, and those that serve an area population of less than 3,000 or 7,000-19,000 all reported lower median figures for 2015 than 2014.

Broken out across all subgroups, library spending on printed children's books varied greatly while again the figures rose consistently with an increase in service area population, staff numbers, and general print book spending. Overall, libraries that spend more than $30,000 on print books spent the most on printed children's books in 2015. Their mean amount was $88,219.33 and their median figure was $27,000 in a range of $5,000-$535,490. In contrast, libraries that spend less than $4,500 on print books spent the least on print children's books in 2015 with a mean of $1,175.50 and a median of $950. Libraries with 1 or less full time equivalent staff members reported the smallest range overall: $0-$3,000.

Print Children's Books Spending in 2016

The participants then provided the figures for their libraries anticipated spending on print children's books in 2016. Of the entire sample, the mean amount libraries predict they will spend on print children's books in 2016 rose to $24,284.65 while the median of $4,250 and range of $0-535,490.00 did not change from the year before. The increase from the prior year was 0.7% or less than 1%.

The results were broken out by service area population. Libraries which serve an area population of less than 3,000 predict they will spend a mean $1,728.63, less than the year before, in a range of $0-$12,000 on print children's books in 2016. For libraries with a service area population of 3,000-7,000 the mean figure was $3,513.33 but their range was just $0-$10,000. Libraries in the 7,000-19,000 population bracket reported a mean of $7,086.67 in a range of $600-$24,000. Finally, libraries with a service area population above 19,000 anticipate they will spend a mean $82,436.88 on printed children's books in 2016. Their reported range was $2,000-$535,490.

Broken out across all subgroups, libraries that spend more than $30,000 anticipate spending the most overall. Their mean amount was $88,732.67 and their median figure was $27,000 in a range of $5,500-$535,490.00. On the other hand, libraries that employ 1 or less full time equivalent staff members anticipate spending the least on printed children's books in 2016. Their mean and median figures were just $1,315.58 and $1,000, respectively. They also reported the narrowest range: $0-$4,000.

Children's eBook Spending in 2014

The next question asked was: What was your library's spending on eBooks intended primarily for children in 2014. Of the entire sample, the mean was $1,879.63 and the median was $0. The minimum amount spent on eBooks for children in 2014 was $0 and the maximum was $73,000.

Broken out across all subgroups, libraries serving an area population of less than 3,000 spent the least on eBooks intended primarily for children in 2014. None of these libraries spent any money on these books. In contrast, libraries with more than 6 full time equivalent staff members spent the most on children's eBooks. These libraries spent a mean $7,567.69 and median $2,000 in a range of $0-$73,000 on these reading materials.

The results were broken out by the libraries spending on print books. The results did not increase in-line with print spending increases as they did before. Libraries that spend between $14,000 and $30,000 on print books spent the lowest mean amount on eBooks intended for children, $100. This figure was in a range of $0-$1,000. Libraries that spend $4,500-$14,000 on print books reported a narrower range, $0-$500, but their mean figure was $124.67. Next, libraries that spend less than $4,500 on print books spent a mean $210, in a range of $0-$3,000. Finally, by spending on print books, libraries that spend more than $30,000 also spent the most on children's eBooks in 2014. They reported a mean of $7,336.92 and were the only bracket to not have a median figure of $0, theirs was $1,100. Their range was $0-$73,000.

Children's eBook Spending in 2015

We then asked the survey participants how much their library had spent on eBooks intended primarily for children in 2015. Predictably, the numbers increased from the year previous. Of the entire sample, the mean was $2,097.06 and the median was $0 in a range of $0-$75,000. The increase was approximately 11.2%.

Broken out across all subcategories, most of the libraries reported a notable increase in their mean spending on children's eBooks from 2014 to 2015 but two groups reported a decrease. Libraries employing 1 or less full time equivalent staff members spent just a mean $45 on eBooks for children in 2015, down from a mean of $62.22 in 2014. Libraries that spend $4,500-$14,000 on print books reported a slightly smaller decrease: a mean of $124, down from $124.66 the year before. Overall, libraries with a service area population of less than 3,000 once again spent the least on eBooks for children: $0. And, once again, libraries with more than 6 full time equivalent employees spent the most: a mean of $8,327.69 and a median of $3,560 in a range of $0-$75,000.

Children's eBook Spending in 2016

To conclude the survey section on spending on eBooks intended primarily for children, we asked the participants what their library's anticipated spending on these materials will be in 2016. As might be expected, the participants anticipate an increase in spending on eBooks for children in 2016. Of the entire sample, the mean was $2,515.09 while the median remained at $0, in a range of $0-$85,000. The increase in the mean is expected to be 19.7%.

The results were broken out by the population of the library service area. Libraries with a service area population of less than 3,000 do anticipate spending money on eBooks for children in 2016. They predicted a mean amount of $16.67 in a range of $0-$250. The mean figures reported by libraries in the other service area population brackets were: $396.43 for those in the 3,000-7,000 range, $850 for those with a population between 7,000 and 19,000 and $9,775 for those with a service area population of more than 19,000.

Once more, libraries employing more than 6 full time equivalent staff members plan on spending the most on eBooks intended for children in 2016, when broken out across all the subgroups. Their predicted mean amount is $10,433.33 and their median is $4,500. They were the only group to not predict a minimum figure of $0. These libraries plan on spending a minimum of $500 and a maximum of $85,000 in 2016 on eBooks for children.

PRINT BOOK CULLING DECISION MAKING

Factors in Print Book Culling Decisions

Our next question was, "What factors does the library take into account when it makes print book culling decisions?" All sixty-two participants responded to this open-ended question. Despite the number of responses, the answers were all quite similar. Two factors were named by almost every single participant: Condition and Circulation. Libraries most often weed out books that are "damaged or in a condition that is unhealthy to circulate" and those that are infrequently checked out. One participant said "Any book that has not circulated in 5 years is removed from the collection, unless it is a classic and in good shape." For another participant it was just 2 years. Other frequently cited factors included the age of the book, its relevancy or how up to date the information contained within is. Some of the less frequently mentioned factors include: attractiveness, the popularity of the author, whether or not it is part of a series the number of copies in stock, space, and cost. Two participants said they use the standard weeding decisions as defined by the CREW manual.

PRINT BOOK COLLECTION VOLUME

Print Book Collection 2014

We then asked the survey participants what the total number of volumes in their library's print book collection was in 2014. Of the entire sample, the mean was 58,325.17 and the median was 21,538.50 in a range of 0-660,000.

The mean and median total number of volumes in the libraries' print book collection consistently rose with the increase in service area population, number of full time equivalent staff members, and spending on print books. Broken out across all the subcategories the library group with the fewest number of print volumes in 2014 were those with a service area population of less than 3,000. Their mean number of volumes was 9,306 and their median was 10,000. The libraries with the most volumes of print books overall were, unsurprisingly, those that spend more than $30,000 on print books. Their mean was 172,305.07 and their median was 60,000 in a range of 30,000-660,000. Across the groups a minimum of 0 was reported by a library with a service area population of less than 3,000, one with 1 or less full time equivalent staff members, and one that spends $4,500-$14,000 on print books. Libraries that spend less than $4,500 on print books reported the second lowest minimum number of volumes in their print book collection: 358.

Print Book Collection 2015

We then asked the participants what the total number of volumes in their library's print book collection was in 2015. There was a slim increase in the overall number of print books in the libraries' collection from 2014-2015. Of the overall sample, in 2015 the mean total number of volumes was 59,399 and the median number was 22,408.5. The minimum number increased to 420 but the maximum for the entire sample dropped to 645,000.

Broken out across all subcategories, only one group reported that their library's print book collection had decreased in size between 2014 and 2015. Libraries that spend less than $4,500 on print books had a mean 11,224.43 and a median 8,500 volumes in their print book collection in 2015, down from 11,388.07 and 9,308.5 the year before. Overall, libraries with a service area population of less than 3,000 reported the lowest mean total number of volumes in their print collection, 10,447.60 in a range of 420-21,817. Libraries that spend more than $30,000 on print books once again had the most volumes, a mean of 175,559.67 and a median 58,000 in a range of 33,000-645,000.

The results were broken out by the libraries' service area populations, illustrating the overall trend towards increasing print book collections and the pattern of increasing figures through the brackets. As previously mentioned the mean number of volumes in the print collection of libraries serving a population of less than 3,000 was 10,447.60. Their reported range was 420-

21,817. Libraries serving a population of 3,000-7,000 had a mean 21,437.33 volumes in a range of 8,000-56,000. Libraries in the next population bracket, serving 7,000-19,000, had a mean number of 29,804.93. Their reported minimum was a slightly lower 5,000 but their maximum was 58,000. Finally, numbers jumped drastically for libraries in the top bracket. These libraries had a mean 166,774.81 volumes in their print collection in 2015. Their median number was 54,900.50 in a range of 18,000 to 245,000.

Print Book Collection 2016

The participants then shared what the anticipated total number of volumes in their library's print book collection will be in 2016. Again, the results show a trend towards increasing overall print book collection numbers. Of the entire sample, the mean was 60,460 and the median was 23,250. The minimum number increased to 450 and the maximum jumped to 700,000.

The results were broken out by the libraries' spending on print books. Libraries that spend less than $4,500 on print books anticipate having a mean 11,321.43 volumes, in a range of 450-5,000, in their print book collection in 2016, the smallest number in this grouping. Once more, libraries that spend more than $30,000 on print books anticipate having the most volumes overall, a mean 179,813.33 in a range of 36,000-700,000. Libraries that spend between $14,000 and $30,000 anticipate a very modest increase in the number of volumes in their print book collection: a mean 29,733.33 in 2016 up from 29,213.20 in 2015. These libraries reported a range of 13,000-54,000. Finally, libraries that spend $4,500-$14,000 were the only ones to anticipate a decrease in the total number of volumes in their print book collection in 2016. They predict having a mean 20,368.78 volumes in 2016, down from 20,950.31 in 2015. Their minimum dropped considerably from 5,000 to just 1,900 while their maximum increased to 59,000 from 56,000.

Across all subgroups, libraries with a service area population of less than 3,000 once more claimed having the smallest collection of print books. Their anticipated mean number of total volumes in their collections in 2016 is just 9,226.67 in a range of 450-22,150.00. They also reported the largest decrease in their collection numbers. Their mean figure dropped by over 1,200 from 10,447.60 in 2015.

Areas of Print Collection Elimination

We then asked the participants to share which areas their libraries have been the most aggressive in eliminating print titles and why these areas were targeted. All sixty-two library representatives responded to this open end question. Non-fiction and reference were the areas most frequently cited; they were named by more than three quarters of the participants. The participants say that these materials become dated and irrelevant quickly and that people turn to digital editions for the most up-to date content. A number of participants also noted that these books are often quite expensive to buy and not budget friendly to replace. Adult and children's fiction were also named by a considerable number of participants. These books are generally culled due to either a lack of popularity/poor circulation or poor condition and to make room on the shelves for new titles. A few of the participants said they do not focus on any one area in particular; they just focus on any outdated, unused, or falling apart materials. A few others said that they do not cull their collections at all.

Changes in Print Collection over the Past Five Years

We then asked the participants, "What has happened to your library's print book collection over the past five years? Is it larger than it was five years ago, in what areas has it grown? If it is smaller, in what areas has it diminished?" Once more, all of the participants address this set of open-ended questions. The responses were quite evenly divided. Twenty-two of the libraries have seen their collections increase, nineteen said they have decreased, and the remaining twenty-one said they had remained the same, mainly due to balancing books out and books in, decreasing in one area while increasing in another. Not all of the participants shared which areas had seen the most change. Of those that did, most said that their non-fiction and reference sections had undergone considerable culling in the past years. Fiction sections (adult, young adult, and children's) were often cited as areas that had seen increases over the past few years. The large print section also grew in a number of the libraries.

Changes in Print Collection over the Next Five Years

To conclude the section on collection volume we asked, "In your view what will happen to your library's print collection over the next five years? Will it become larger or smaller? What areas will be most affected and why? Will spending remain the same?" All sixty-two of the participants responded to this series of questions. For most the answer was no change.

More than 40% of the respondents anticipate the size of their print book collection will remain the same over the next five years. Again, this is largely due to a careful balance of matching books in with books out and often decreasing the numbers in a particular section while increasing those in another. The remaining participants were fairly evenly divided between anticipating an overall increase to their print collection and predicting it would become smaller. Once more, participants frequently said that non-fiction and the reference section would be the areas that saw the most significant decrease in print numbers. A large number of the participants mentioned increasing their eBook collection.

Most of the participants do not anticipate any real changes to their spending either. Of the twenty-nine participants that addressed that part of the question, sixteen said they believed their spending would stay the same. A more optimistic eight participants are hopeful that their spending and budgets will increase in the coming years. Of those that mentioned decreases in spending, reduced funding from "the city" was the most often cited cause.

PRINT BOOK CULLING STRATEGY

Percentage Culled in Past Year

"Approximately what percentage of your print book collection did you cull in the past year?" was the next question we asked the survey participants. Of the entire sample, the mean figure was 12.36% and the median was 8% in a range of 1%-100%.

Broken out by the libraries' service area populations, those serving less than 3,000 culled the greatest percentage of books from their print collection in the past year. They culled a mean 20.21% and a median 10%. These libraries claimed the maximum 100% while they were also the only ones to not claim a minimum of 1%; they culled a minimum 3%. Libraries serving an area population of 7,000-19,000 and more than 19,000 also culled a median 10% of their print books last year. For the former group the mean was 11.04% in a range of 1%-50% while for the latter it was a slightly higher 11.35% in a narrower 1%-30% range. Finally, libraries with a service area population of 3,000-7,000 culled the lowest percentage of books from their print collection in the last year, a mean of just 7.20% and a median of 5% in a range of 1%-20%.

The results were further broken out by the libraries' spending on print book collections. Libraries that spend the least on their print book collections culled the highest percentage of print books in the past year. They removed a mean 20.43% of the volumes in their collection, in a range of 3%-100%. On the other hand, libraries that spend the second lowest amount, $4,500-$14,000 culled the lowest percentage of books, a mean 7.73% in a range of 1%-30%. In the middle, libraries that spend between $14,000 and $30,000 on print books culled a mean 8.97% in a slim range of 1%-20% and those that spend the most, over $30,000, culled a sizeable mean 12.95% in a range of 1%-50%.

Changes in Acquisition and Culling Strategy

We then wanted to know if the libraries had changed their book acquisition and/or culling strategy over the past five years, or if they expect to change it soon. We asked the participants to describe these changes. Of the entire sample, just 52 participants responded and 30 of those said that they had made no changes to their acquisition or culling strategy.

Of those who had made changes the most frequently cited adjustment to the libraries' culling or acquisition strategy was a more aggressive approach to "weeding." One participant stated: "The library moved to an ongoing three year weeding schedule. The general rule of thumb is for every six new books added to the collection we expect to weed 5." Another participant said, "We used to cull only books that were badly damaged or hadn't been circulated in 5 years. I now cull more frequently based on what interests and needs I see in our patrons." A number of participants said that they had moved to the CREW method of culling while another said they are using "Collection HQ reports to more aggressively weed." Space considerations and weeding out sources of outdated information were the most frequently cited reasons for changing culling strategy.

A few of the participants also mentioned changes made to their book acquisition strategy. Some of these changes included: supplying what the patrons want, increasing the budget for fiction books, and adding or shifting to eBooks.

Future Changes in Print Book Acquisition and Culling

Continuing to explore culling and acquisition strategy, we posed the following questions to the participants: "In what areas do you believe that the library will be most aggressive in culling print books in the future? In what areas or subjects do you believe that the library is likely to increase spending on print books?" We received 60 responses to this pair of questions but a number were not helpful as participants named library sections without specifying whether the changes anticipated were in culling or increasing spending.

Once more, non-fiction collections were the focus of the most culling plans due to unused and outdated material. Many participants also said that they would continue to weed out their adult and juvenile fiction, keeping with their established culling schedules in these areas. "Old tatty children's books" and audio books were also proposed targets of future aggressive culls.

Most of the participants said that they do not foresee any considerable increases in print book spending in the near future. Still a number of participants are hopeful that they will have more funds available to spend on their print collections. Despite being the popular target for aggressive culling, a few of the participants did say that they plan on increasing their non-fiction holdings in a few key areas: self-help, DIY home projects, cookbooks, art and history etc. Print book fiction collections- adult, young adult, and children's- are where most participants anticipate they will increase their spending in the future. Large print collections were also named a number of times; one participant said, "Most of our additional print spending will be on large print books—this area is by far our fastest growing demand area." Christian fiction and locally authored fiction were two specialty collections that were also identified as areas where spending may be increased.

SPACE ISSUES

Increasing Space for Other Uses

Next we asked about changes in the use of library space. We asked the participants, "If the library has reduced the size of its book collection in recent years, has this led to an increase in space that the library can use for other purposes?" Of the entire sample, 33.87% said that culling print books had freed up space for other purposes in their libraries. 59.68% answered the question with "no" and the remaining 6.45% did not provide an answer.

The greatest variance in responses is seen when the results are broken out by the libraries' spending on print books. At the very bottom of the group, just 6.67% of libraries that spend between $14,000 and $30,000 on print books said that they had increased space for other purposes by reducing the size of their print collection. Next were libraries that spend less than $4,500. Jumping considerably, a substantial 37.5% of these libraries said they had increased library space for other purposes. Despite only culling a mean 7.73% of their print volumes in the last year, libraries that spend $4,500-$14,000 on print books said they had changed their use of library space, increasing space for other purposes through reducing the size of its book collection, at a rate of 43.75%. Finally, 46.67% of libraries that spend over $30,000 on print books saw changes to their use of space through the reduction of print book collections.

Changes in Space over the Past 5 Years

We then wanted to know, if the libraries have had space freed-up over the past five years, how much space has been made available and how was it being used? Of the entire sample, just forty-three participants responded to this open-ended question. More than a quarter of the participants that did respond said that they had not freed-up any space in the past five years. For many the only space that had been made available through culling collections was additional shelf space. This space is used for new books or to more effectively and attractively arrange current holdings.

While few of the participants specified the amount of space they have managed to free-up in recent years the details of their use of the newly available space show that some freed up very little space while others repurposed significantly larger areas. That most have only freed up shelf space suggests that a large percentage of the space increases were on the smaller side. Still, one participant now has "a small seating area with a table" while another said "We have created sitting and group study areas, added two research sections and created a storytime zone as well as creating dedicated spaces for computers, laptops and printing." Increasing patron seating; expanding or adding study, meeting and computer areas; and making space for programs and activities were some of the other more frequently named uses for newly available space in the libraries.

OPINION OF LIBRARY PATRONS ON PRINT VS. DIGITAL

Survey of Print vs. Digital Preferences

Our next topic of inquiry was whether or not the libraries had surveyed their patrons on their preferences for print vs. digital resources as a prelude to decision making on reducing the size of their book collections. Of the entire sample, just 27.42% said they had conducted such a survey; 72.58% said they had not.

The tendency to survey patrons was not particularly library size dependent. On one end of the spectrum, just 6.67% of libraries that spend $14,000-$30,000 on print books surveyed their patrons on their preferences for print vs. digital resources before making decisions about reducing the size of their print collections. At the other end, 50% of libraries that spend between $4,500 and $14,000, those that made the fewest reductions, surveyed their patrons. This was the largest percentage overall. In the middle, 12.5% of libraries that spend less than $4,500 on print books and a considerable 40% of those that spend more than $30,000 surveyed their patrons about their resource preferences before making changes to their collections.

The results were further broken out by population of the library service area. Once again this measure of library size did not explain any differences in the percentage of libraries that surveyed their patrons. The percentages that did survey their patrons were: 25% of those that serve less than 3,000, 26.67% of both those serving populations of 3,000-7,000 and 7,000-19,000 and 31.25% of those serving an area population of over 19,000.

Friends of the Library Opinions on Spending on Print vs. Digital Books

We then asked the survey participants to share their Friends of the Library organizations' opinions on the use of library resources for increased spending on print or eBooks. Of the entire sample, just 1.61% said their Friends of the Library group tends to be more supportive of eBooks, 20.97% said they tend to be more supportive of print books, and a majority 70.97% said they do not really take a position on the issue. The remaining 6.45% did not provide an answer.

The results were broken out by the libraries' service area population. Libraries with a service area population of more than 19,000 accounted for all of the libraries that indicated that their Friends of the Library organizations tend to be more supportive of spending on eBooks than on print books. Even for this group, however, only 6.25% noted that their Friends of the Library organization were more supportive of print than eBooks and 25% of these libraries said their Friends of the Library organizations favour increased spending on print books while the remaining 62.5% said they do not really take a position on the issue. Of the remaining groups, 25% of libraries serving an area population of less than 3,000 also say their Friends of the Library organizations tend to be more supportive of print books, as do 20% of those serving 7,000-19,000 and 13.33% of those serving 3,000-7,000.

Local School District Preferences

We asked if the local school districts in the library's service area tend to want the library to prioritize eBooks or print books in the library's purchasing decisions or if they do not have a preference. Of the entire sample, just 3.23% said they believe the local school districts tend to favour eBooks while 17.74% prioritize print books in library purchasing decisions. 77.24% said they do not seem to have a preference and the remaining 1.61% did not answer the question.

Again, the results were broken out by the libraries' service area populations. 6.25% of both libraries serving an area population of less than 3,000 and more than 19,000 said their local school districts seem to prioritize eBooks in library spending decisions. 12.5% of the former group and 18.75% of the latter said they seem to prioritize spending on print books, and the remainder noted that there did not seem to be any preference. None of the libraries with a service area population of 3,000-7,000 and 7,000-19,000 said their local school districts seem to prefer eBooks while 20% of both said they prioritize print books in library purchasing decisions.

CULLED MATERIALS HANDLING

Use of Offsite Storage

Next we asked the survey participants if their library uses offsite storage for books, journals and other printed materials. Of the entire sample, a majority 95.16% said they do not while just 4.84% said they do.

The results were broken out by the population of the libraries service area. None of the libraries with a service area population of 7,000-19,000 use offsite storage for books, journals and other printed materials. Libraries that have a service area population of 3,000-7,000 are the most likely to use offsite storage; 6.67% said they do. In the middle, 6.25% of both libraries which serve an area population of less than 3,000 and more than 19,000 say they store their print materials offsite.

Changes in Offsite Storage Space Use and Cost

Further exploring the topic of offsite storage, we asked: "Has the amount of space used for offsite storage increased or decreased in recent years and if so by how much? Also what has been the trend in storage costs?" Most of the participants responded to this open-ended set questions with "N/A" and one said "We do not have off-site storage; we have very little storage in the library either. If we don't have room for it, we don't have it."

In total, we received just three responses about the libraries' use of offsite storage. One participant from a library with a service area population of less than 3,000 said their storage needs have greatly increased and their offsite storage consists of the "attic of the community building," while other materials are stored in the library basement. This participant said that there are "no monetary costs to store" but the community organization doesn't like sharing their attic space and it has "stirred some animosity." One of the participants from a library with a service area population of more than 19,000 said "Storage costs are up and it's hard to find adequate storage nearby. We plan to use offsite storage more to house seasonal collections that we don't want to warehouse on the shelves in our libraries." Finally another representative from a library in the largest service area population bracket said that they have moved their offsite storage of historical furnishings to their onsite garage. They did not say why they stopped using offsite storage.

Data Use and Print Material Culling Decision Making

We wanted to know what kinds of data the libraries use in making print material culling decisions and how the different data sets contribute to their decision making. Many of the survey participants responded to this open-ended question by naming some of the previously discussed factors they take into consideration when making culling decisions: the books' condition, circulation statistics, relevance, availability within the system, age and copy write date etc. Seven of the fifty-three participants who answered this question said they use the CREW manual or method. CREW was developed by the Texas State Library and Archives Commission and uses the MUSTIE acronym: "Misleading, Ugly, Superseded, Trivial, Irrelevant, E=the material may be obtained expeditiously Elsewhere through ILL or otherwise."

Some of the libraries do not use any data when making culling decisions and many rely solely on their librarians' expertise, experience, and knowledge. For others, programs can be helpful. Specific programs used to access data on circulation and usage that the participants named were: Book System, Collection HQ and Sirsi. A number of participants also said they use the library's own ILS which can provide them with circulation information. Using a combination of intuition, observation, and usage reports seems to be the best approach to print material culling decision making.

Giving Away Culled Books

We asked the participants what percentage of their culled book collection is given away to schools, libraries, charitable agencies or other venues. Of the entire sample, the mean was 46.61% and the median was 50% in a range of 0%-100%.

Once again the results were broken out by the size of the library's service area population. Libraries serving a population of more than 19,000 were the most likely to donate their culled books to schools, other libraries, charitable agencies or other venues; a majority 56.14%, mean, do. They were the only libraries not to report a minimum of 0%; their range was 2%-100%. On the other hand, libraries serving an area population of 3,000-7,000 were the least likely to give away their culled books. A mean of just 33.92% of these libraries donate their books. Their median figure was just 15% compared to 65% of those serving more than 19,000. In the middle, a mean 46.32% and median 50% of libraries with a service area population of 7,000-19,000 and a mean 48.32% and median 50% of those with a service area population of less than 3,000 also give away their culled books.

Restoring Access to Culled Print Materials

To conclude this section of the survey, we asked the participants to mention some incidents, if any, in which the library was forced to back track and restore access to print copies of materials that had been culled in print form. Nineteen participants shared instances of this happening in their libraries. Books that have been culled due to poor condition are often replaced and occasionally a fiction book that was not circulating well will all of a sudden become popular and need to be brought back into circulation. According to our participants, print materials that had been culled and needed to be replaced were most often books that were part of a series, classics, or ones that were made into a movie.

Another reason to restore access to culled print material is patrons changing format preferences. One participant said "We really cut down on our magazine subscriptions as people went to digital editions. Now we are seeing more patrons ask for print magazines again." Some of the other instances which have forced the libraries to back track and restore access to materials that had been culled include: "a book group chooses an older book and there are not enough copies in the system," books appearing on "The Battle of the Books List," and "the [culled] book was left on the shelf and patron has brought it up to the check out."

SUPPORT FOR PRINT OR DIGITAL

Library Users who Prefer Print

Next we wanted to know if the participants felt there were any particular types of library users more likely to prefer print and lobby the library for more spending on print books. Who are these users? We received 57 responses to this open ended question. A number of the participants said that there was no one type of user who preferred print. As one respondent shared, "The users are all ages, genders....The usage reports from my eBook provider show .8% of cardholders are eBook users at my library." Echoing this appraisal, many participants said that either all or most of their patrons preferred print materials.

Participants did identify some particular types of library users who are more likely to prefer print and lobby for more spending on print books. Overwhelmingly, the most frequently named specific type of library users were seniors or older library patrons. The next most frequently identified specific group were the parents of young children. As one participant said, "Parents find a picture book more satisfying to hold and explore than an eReader or tablet." Other specific types of library users who prefer print that the participants identified were: long time library users, patrons who cannot afford an electronic reading device, avid readers, those who like the feel of books in their hands, "users who actually come into the library," and "those patrons who choose not to read on electronic reading devices." One participant said that "no one lobbies for more books."

Print Collection Culling Organization and Decision Making

We then asked, "How is print collection culling at your library organized? Which librarians are involved in the decision-making? Who makes the final decisions in particular areas? Who reviews decisions? Who overturns decisions?" Fifty-seven participants responded to this series of open-ended questions. Based on the size of the libraries and their staff, the results varied greatly.

First, nine of the participants addressed the issue of how print culling is organized, in terms of frequency and culling criteria, at their respective libraries. As we have seen in the answers to many previous questions the decision to cull a particular book is arrived at by considering the age, condition, and circulation of the book. One library keeps an ongoing list of books to be culled while others have specific culling periods. Frequency of culling sessions can vary from as needed, to "no less than 2-3 times a year," to yearly or every three years.

Many more participants shared who the individuals responsible for organizing print collection culling and making, reviewing and overturning decisions at their library are. Again, depending on the size of the library and its staff it could be a very simple streamlined operation or quite complex. On the one hand, many of the libraries, particularly those with a service area population of less than 3,000, said they only have one employee and that employee is the sole decision maker when it comes to print collection culling. Similarly, ten of the participants said their library director takes care of the entire culling process. When they were not responsible for the entire production directors were often named as the figures responsible for reviewing and finalizing all print collection culling decisions made by other staff members. Most frequently, the participants said that the print collection culling at their library was a collaborative effort. Sometimes this means two or more employees working together on the library's entire collection or more often multiple librarians or managers from specific departments decide which materials to cull from their respective collections.

Mistakes in Print Book Collection Development

Our next question was: "What is the greatest mistake that the library has made in its print book collection development decision making in recent years?" More than half of the participants shared their library's greatest mistake in collection development with us, though a number were eager to point out that the mistakes were the fault of previous employees. Some of the most common mistakes listed were: getting rid of books just to have them requested again, ordering either too many or too few copies of a particular book, struggling to work within the budget, weeding too aggressively, and purchasing books just because they won awards or made a bestsellers list or "just in case someone may want to read it." A number of the participants mentioned that they had particular problems with their young adult and middle school purchases; they have trouble gauging the interest of their readers, buying the right titles, keeping up with changes, building readership and getting "teens interested in anything but computer games." Two of the most standout answers we received were: "The most controversial decision was to not add *50 Shades of Grey* to the collection" and "We don't make mistakes, unless it is buying books by Glen Beck!!"

Advice

Finally, we asked the survey participants if they have any advice for their peers on planning for the future in public library book purchasing. Forty-seven participants offered up hints for future success. Overwhelmingly, one piece of advice was given time and time again: know your patrons and their wants! As one participant said, I believe any library has to tailor their collection for the patrons in the area they serve." To do so, libraries must "listen and watch what your patrons are checking out and their interests." Participants suggested listening to patrons' requests, surveying users, and paying close attention to their indicated needs and desires. In the words of one participant: "Learn from your patron, what they like to read and purchase then."

Participants had other bits of advice to offer: stick to your budget and get more funding, utilize a good circulation data tool, do your research, read reviews, balance your purchases throughout the library, weed smartly, and be flexible: "Take a deep breath and accept change."

ALTERNATIVES TO PRINT

How comfortable would you say your library is with the substitution of eBooks for print books? When does the acquisition of an eBook title lead you to eliminate or reduce your holdings of the print version of the same title? Broken out by Population of Library Service Area

DEFINED BY SIZE OF SERVICE AREA
Less than 3000
1) n/a
2) Not comfortable. Most of our patrons vastly prefer print books.
3) not much, people still want print books...we do overdrive with other libraries
4) Not ready to make transition yet. Contribute only $100 towards e-books which are purchased by library system
5) Not comfortable
6) Not yet comfortable.
7) do not use e books
8) Our patronage is mostly geriatric and preschool. EBooks aren't much of an issue.
9) We don't have any eBooks.
10) Uncomfortable right now, we currently do not have an e-reader for the public to use. Finances are not allowing this in our mega budget.
11) 0
12) We don't have E-Books yet.
13) We do not eliminate a title if we have an e book. Many of our patrons cannot access eBooks.
14) The library is not comfortable with eBooks. I would not eliminate a print book just because I had it as an eBook.
15) We do not substitute eBooks for print books. The library does not directly purchase eBooks but it a member of a state consortium.
16) we don't do any eBooks

3000+ -7000
1) We carry both versions, have not replaced any titles with virtual copies
2) Not very - we haven't yet begun to offer e-books
3) We have just joined a consortium to offer eBooks to our constituents. We will probably not duplicate but at the same time print books are still our primary focus.
4) We do not carry eBooks
5) We buy both. Two different type of patrons use eBooks and print copies.
6) The library does not substitute eBooks for print. The acquisition of eBooks does not eliminate or reduce the holdings of the print version of the same title.
7) Currently do not weed books for this reason.

8) I don't buy as many non-fiction and reference books, so the funds from that collection has gone for eBooks. I do duplicate bestsellers, but there are also unique eBook titles that are not published in print.

9) We are comfortable with eBooks. We aren't able to eliminate our holdings of popular materials because of the demand

10) When the demand for eBooks gets greater than the demand for print editions.

11) We don't currently have them, but have raised around $500 in donations this last year to put towards the purchase of what we need to start next fiscal year.

12) Just beginning the comfort journey and haven't given any consideration to reducing the holdings of print for eBooks.

13) Somewhat comfortable. Check-outs are slow but stable. The majority of my patrons are still very comfortable in checking out print version titles.

14) Not comfortable at all. We do not purchase eBooks.

7000-19000

1) We are happy to include eBooks, as it is a service that our patrons are requesting. However, I feel that the cost of eBooks for libraries is much higher than it needs to be. There are also more licensing stipulations placed on eBooks for libraries, making it hard for us to provide everything that patron want. Thus, we have a service that isn't the best it can be, and it's frustrating for patrons to see eBooks available, but not available at their local library, simply because there is no way for us to license the title. EBooks are an important part of the material selection, but there will always be people who want to read print titles instead. We look at computer screens all day, and people are craving a break for their eyes. We likely won't reduce our holdings of print versions. That being said, we have had to reallocate budgets in order to purchase Etitles as well.

2) They are two separate collections - we budget for the consortium eBooks and then budget for print books and we can't bargain between them after the budget is made.

3) The transition is going slowly. We get eBooks through a statewide consortia--print versions are not impacted.

4) Fairly comfortable. Rarely eliminate print version upon acquisition of eBook. Like to have both options available.

5) will retain print copy

6) This has not occurred

7) We have been unable to use e-books due to budgetary limitations

8) WE are very comfortable in purchasing eBooks. The only time we buy and eBook and not a print version is Mass market paperbacks, or eBook only titles.

9) We do not eliminate a print version just because we may have an eBook for that same title.

10) Only when the print version has not been circulated in quite some time. We often have both the print book and the eBook.

11) We use the state overdrive system. It is not a large part of our circulation. At this point our library does not purchase individual eBook titles; additional copies are purchased at the system level based on number of holds for our system. I can't see the number of e-book holds generated by my patrons, so I continued to purchase number of copies based on holds for the print versions. But, I am purchasing more duplicate copies than I have in the past because of print copy holds.

12) We do not have eBook holdings

13) The users of eBooks and print books are different. In our case the use of eBooks has doubled from 475/month in 2013 to 875/month in 2015.

14) Not comfortable at all. We are a part of a larger consortium that chooses materials on our behalf - our print choices are not coordinated with eBooks acquisitions.

15) No comfortable with substitution but with purchasing both.

More than 19000

1) As a rural public library, our number one format is still print. We purpose eBooks as an additional format, not to replace existing.

2) We are very comfortable with the substitution of eBooks. We don't usually weed our print books based on eBooks holdings though.

3) We currently buy eBooks in addition to print, not instead of for new titles. For older titles we may buy the eBook version so that we don't need to make room on our shelves for the print copy of a title that may not circ more than once or twice a year.

4) Staff is comfortable with it but cost and patrons needs don't make it logical. Print will always have priority due to economic status of patrons.

5) We make eBooks available but do not substitute. Our book circulation remains very much higher than eBook circ.

6) In our situation, eBooks are available for many books. We share with a consortium of 27 public libraries. We buy the print book over the eBook as most of our customers do not own readers or tablets. We are in a small, rural library with an older population.

7) Fairly comfortable. Our reference and magazine areas are quickly being replaced by ematerials; in areas of general interest we tend to have both of the most popular items; older items (like series, romance, westerns, etc.) we rely on eBooks rather than replace hard copies.

8) EBooks don't eliminate print books, but they might become the majority of duplicate copies.

9) Not yet - but it can substitute for some of the additional copies we might purchase to satisfy borrower requests

10) We are currently purchasing in both and have not eliminated or reduced holdings of print holdings.

11) Our library is completely comfortable with the interchangeability of print and digital. We often reduce the number of copies of a title we will acquire if we have unlimited access to the same title in digital. Conversely, we often purchase a print copies of a popular digital title.

12) We are still only buying print books. We do have a subscription to the state wide e-book database.

13) We would not replace a book in print with a digital title, it is considered an added format and not a replacement format. Our primary circulation is through print and only 10% is in digital format.

14) We are building an e collection but that does not negate the necessity of having print books or books on CD, MPS, etc.

15) I do not substitute eBooks for print. The acquisition of an eBook never leads me to eliminate print holdings. In the past, I have added older books in a series on eBook as a replacement or filling in of the print items.

Table 1 How much did your library spend on eBooks in each of the following years?

Table 1.1.1 How much did your library spend on eBooks in 2014? (All figures in $ US)

	Mean	Median	Minimum	Maximum
Entire sample	10499,97	650,00	0,00	273000,00

Table 1.1.2 How much did your library spend on eBooks in 2014? (All figures in $ US) Broken out by Population of Library Service Area

Population of Library Service Area	Mean	Median	Minimum	Maximum
Less than 3000	120,00	0,00	0,00	500,00
3000+ -7000	896,20	0,00	0,00	4743,00
7000-19000	2089,87	1500,00	0,00	10000,00
More than 19000	37119,19	8250,00	0,00	273000,00

Table 1.1.3 How much did your library spend on eBooks in 2014? (All figures in $ US) Broken out by Size of full time equivalent library staff

Size of full time equivalent library staff	Mean	Median	Minimum	Maximum
1 or less	211,11	0,00	0,00	1500,00
1+ -2.8	438,31	0,00	0,00	2500,00
2.8+ -6	2835,71	1350,00	0,00	20707,00
More than 6	36956,25	8250,00	500,00	273000,00

Table 1.1.4 How much did your library spend on eBooks in 2014? (All figures in $ US) Broken out by Spending on print books ($)

Spending on print books ($)	Mean	Median	Minimum	Maximum
Less than 4500	540,00	0,00	0,00	6000,00
4500-14000	659,25	400,00	0,00	2500,00
14000-30000	2456,67	1000,00	0,00	20707,00
More than 30000	39000,00	8500,00	500,00	273000,00

Public Library Plans for the Book Collection

Table 1.2.1 How much did your library spend on eBooks in 2015? (All figures in $ US)

	Mean	Median	Minimum	Maximum
Entire sample	12949,33	1000,00	0,00	275000,00

Table 1.2.2 How much did your library spend on eBooks in 2015? (All figures in $ US) Broken out by Population of Library Service Area

Population of Library Service Area	Mean	Median	Minimum	Maximum
Less than 3000	170,00	0,00	0,00	500,00
3000+ -7000	1006,80	500,00	0,00	5902,00
7000-19000	2089,00	1500,00	0,00	8000,00
More than 19000	46307,63	15500,00	0,00	275000,00

Table 1.2.3 How much did your library spend on eBooks in 2015? (All figures in $ US) Broken out by Size of full time equivalent library staff

Size of full time equivalent library staff	Mean	Median	Minimum	Maximum
1 or less	197,22	0,00	0,00	1500,00
1+ -2.8	669,85	500,00	0,00	2500,00
2.8+ -6	3794,57	1500,00	0,00	29372,00
More than 6	45282,94	9500,00	1200,00	275000,00

Table 1.2.4 How much did your library spend on eBooks in 2015? (All figures in $ US) Broken out by Spending on print books ($)

Spending on print books ($)	Mean	Median	Minimum	Maximum
Less than 4500	673,33	0,00	0,00	8000,00
4500-14000	706,75	500,00	0,00	2500,00
14000-30000	3596,73	1500,00	0,00	29372,00
More than 30000	47636,67	11000,00	0,00	275000,00

Public Library Plans for the Book Collection

Table 1.3.1 How much will your library spend on eBooks in 2016 (anticipated)? (All figures in $ US)

	Mean	Median	Minimum	Maximum
Entire sample	14989,92	1200,00	0,00	300000,00

Table 1.3.2 How much will your library spend on eBooks in 2016 (anticipated)? (All figures in $ US) Broken out by Population of Library Service Area

Population of Library Service Area	Mean	Median	Minimum	Maximum
Less than 3000	203,33	0,00	0,00	1000,00
3000+ -7000	1280,00	1200,00	0,00	6000,00
7000-19000	2495,67	1800,00	0,00	8000,00
More than 19000	53418,75	22500,00	500,00	300000,00

Table 1.3.3 How much will your library spend on eBooks in 2016 (anticipated)? (All figures in $ US) Broken out by Size of full time equivalent library staff

Size of full time equivalent library staff	Mean	Median	Minimum	Maximum
1 or less	308,33	50,00	0,00	1500,00
1+ -2.8	845,00	985,00	0,00	3000,00
2.8+ -6	4467,86	1900,00	0,00	35000,00
More than 6	52206,25	16000,00	1200,00	300000,00

Table 1.3.4 How much will your library spend on eBooks in 2016 (anticipated)? (All figures in $ US) Broken out by Spending on print books ($)

Spending on print books ($)	Mean	Median	Minimum	Maximum
Less than 4500	773,33	0,00	0,00	8000,00
4500-14000	817,81	500,00	0,00	3000,00
14000-30000	4200,00	2000,00	0,00	35000,00
More than 30000	55113,33	20000,00	1200,00	300000,00

CHILDREN'S BOOKS

Table 2 What was your library's spending on print children's books in each of the following years?

Table 2.1.1 What was your library's spending on print children's books in 2014? (All figures in $ US)

	Mean	Median	Minimum	Maximum
Entire sample	22803,28	4645,50	0,00	512500,00

Table 2.1.2 What was your library's spending on print children's books in 2014? (All figures in $ US) Broken out by Population of Library Service Area

Population of Library Service Area	Mean	Median	Minimum	Maximum
Less than 3000	1902,81	1050,00	0,00	10000,00
3000+ -7000	3263,64	2943,00	0,00	10000,00
7000-19000	6766,47	7006,00	600,00	19000,00
More than 19000	77056,69	17203,50	2000,00	512500,00

Table 2.1.3 What was your library's spending on print children's books in 2014? (All figures in $ US) Broken out by Size of full time equivalent library staff

Size of full time equivalent library staff	Mean	Median	Minimum	Maximum
1 or less	1444,47	1000,00	0,00	4500,00
1+ -2.8	3921,15	3000,00	0,00	10000,00
2.8+ -6	6420,26	6503,00	1200,00	12407,00
More than 6	77843,75	20500,00	6000,00	512500,00

Public Library Plans for the Book Collection

Table 2.1.4 What was your library's spending on print children's books in 2014? (All figures in $ US) Broken out by Spending on print books ($)

Spending on print books ($)	Mean	Median	Minimum	Maximum
Less than 4500	1412,19	925,00	0,00	9000,00
4500-14000	3314,44	3775,00	0,00	8000,00
14000-30000	6910,00	8000,00	2000,00	12407,00
More than 30000	82301,84	22000,00	5527,64	512500,00

Table 2.2.1 What was your library's spending on print children's books in 2015? (All figures in $ US)

	Mean	Median	Minimum	Maximum
Entire sample	24114,29	4250,00	0,00	535490,00

Table 2.2.2 What was your library's spending on print children's books in 2015? (All figures in $ US) Broken out by Population of Library Service Area

Population of Library Service Area	Mean	Median	Minimum	Maximum
Less than 3000	1738,00	1000,00	0,00	12000,00
3000+ -7000	3331,93	3000,00	0,00	9160,00
7000-19000	6887,13	6600,00	600,00	24000,00
More than 19000	82124,50	19500,00	1800,00	535490,00

Table 2.2.3 What was your library's spending on print children's books in 2015? (All figures in $ US) Broken out by Size of full time equivalent library staff

Size of full time equivalent library staff	Mean	Median	Minimum	Maximum
1 or less	1226,74	1000,00	0,00	3000,00
1+ -2.8	3758,46	2500,00	0,00	12000,00
2.8+ -6	6402,00	6553,50	1200,00	10000,00
More than 6	83330,63	25500,00	5000,00	535490,00

Table 2.2.4 What was your library's spending on print children's books in 2015? (All figures in $ US) Broken out by Spending on print books ($)

Spending on print books ($)	Mean	Median	Minimum	Maximum
Less than 4500	1175,50	950,00	0,00	7000,00
4500-14000	2931,69	2350,00	0,00	8000,00
14000-30000	7072,07	8000,00	2000,00	12000,00
More than 30000	88219,33	27000,00	5000,00	535490,00

Table 2.3.1 What will be your library's spending on print children's books in 2016 (anticipated)? (All figures in $ US)

	Mean	Median	Minimum	Maximum
Entire sample	24284,65	4250,00	0,00	535490,00

Table 2.3.2 What will be your library's spending on print children's books in 2016 (anticipated)? (All figures in $ US) Broken out by Population of Library Service Area

Population of Library Service Area	Mean	Median	Minimum	Maximum
Less than 3000	1728,63	1000,00	0,00	12000,00
3000+ -7000	3513,33	4000,00	0,00	10000,00
7000-19000	7086,67	6600,00	600,00	24000,00
More than 19000	82436,88	19500,00	2000,00	535490,00

Table 2.3.3 What will be your library's spending on print children's books in 2016 (anticipated)? (All figures in $ US) Broken out by Size of full time equivalent library staff

Size of full time equivalent library staff	Mean	Median	Minimum	Maximum
1 or less	1313,58	1000,00	0,00	4000,00
1+ -2.8	3869,23	2500,00	0,00	12000,00
2.8+ -6	6421,43	6600,00	1200,00	10500,00
More than 6	83780,63	25500,00	6000,00	535490,00

Table 2.3.4 What will be your library's spending on print children's books in 2016 (anticipated)? (All figures in $ US) Broken out by Spending on print books ($)

Spending on print books ($)	Mean	Median	Minimum	Maximum
Less than 4500	1334,88	1000,00	0,00	7000,00
4500-14000	2918,75	2250,00	0,00	8000,00
14000-30000	7106,67	8000,00	2000,00	12000,00
More than 30000	88732,67	27000,00	5500,00	535490,00

Table 3 What was your library's spending on eBooks intended primarily for children in each of the following years:

Table 3.1.1 What was your library's spending on eBooks intended primarily for children in 2014? (All figures in $ US)

	Mean	Median	Minimum	Maximum
Entire sample	1879,63	0,00	0,00	73000,00

Table 3.1.2 What was your library's spending on eBooks intended primarily for children in 2014? (All figures in $ US) Broken out by Population of Library Service Area

Population of Library Service Area	Mean	Median	Minimum	Maximum
Less than 3000	0,00	0,00	0,00	0,00
3000+ -7000	132,14	0,00	0,00	1000,00
7000-19000	420,83	125,00	0,00	3000,00
More than 19000	7276,92	1100,00	0,00	73000,00

Table 3.1.3 What was your library's spending on eBooks intended primarily for children in 2014? (All figures in $ US) Broken out by Size of full time equivalent library staff

Size of full time equivalent library staff	Mean	Median	Minimum	Maximum
1 or less	62,22	0,00	0,00	1000,00
1+ -2.8	57,69	0,00	0,00	400,00
2.8+ -6	125,00	0,00	0,00	500,00
More than 6	7567,69	2000,00	0,00	73000,00

Public Library Plans for the Book Collection

Table 3.1.4 What was your library's spending on eBooks intended primarily for children in 2014? (All figures in $ US) Broken out by Spending on print books ($)

Spending on print books ($)	Mean	Median	Minimum	Maximum
Less than 4500	210,00	0,00	0,00	3000,00
4500-14000	124,67	0,00	0,00	500,00
14000-30000	100,00	0,00	0,00	1000,00
More than 30000	7336,92	1100,00	0,00	73000,00

Table 3.2.1 What was your library's spending on eBooks intended primarily for children in 2015? (All figures in $ US)

	Mean	Median	Minimum	Maximum
Entire sample	2097,06	0,00	0,00	75000,00

Table 3.2.2 What was your library's spending on eBooks intended primarily for children in 2015? (All figures in $ US) Broken out by Population of Library Service Area

Population of Library Service Area	Mean	Median	Minimum	Maximum
Less than 3000	0,00	0,00	0,00	0,00
3000+ -7000	226,50	0,00	0,00	1121,00
7000-19000	683,33	150,00	0,00	4500,00
More than 19000	7836,15	3000,00	0,00	75000,00

Table 3.2.3 What was your library's spending on eBooks intended primarily for children in 2015? (All figures in $ US) Broken out by Size of full time equivalent library staff

Size of full time equivalent library staff	Mean	Median	Minimum	Maximum
1 or less	45,00	0,00	0,00	700,00
1+ -2.8	100,00	0,00	0,00	500,00
2.8+ -6	287,10	125,00	0,00	1121,00
More than 6	8327,69	3560,00	0,00	75000,00

Public Library Plans for the Book Collection

Table 3.2.4 What was your library's spending on eBooks intended primarily for children in 2015? (All figures in $ US) Broken out by Spending on print books ($)

Spending on print books ($)	Mean	Median	Minimum	Maximum
Less than 4500	313,33	0,00	0,00	4500,00
4500-14000	124,00	0,00	0,00	500,00
14000-30000	265,55	0,00	0,00	1121,00
More than 30000	7981,54	3000,00	0,00	75000,00

Table 3.3.1 What will be your library's spending on eBooks intended primarily for children in 2016 (anticipated)? (All figures in $ US)

	Mean	Median	Minimum	Maximum
Entire sample	2515,09	0,00	0,00	85000,00

Table 3.3.2 What will be your library's spending on eBooks intended primarily for children in 2016 (anticipated)? (All figures in $ US) Broken out by Population of Library Service Area

Population of Library Service Area	Mean	Median	Minimum	Maximum
Less than 3000	16,67	0,00	0,00	250,00
3000+ -7000	396,43	0,00	0,00	2000,00
7000-19000	850,00	225,00	0,00	5000,00
More than 19000	9775,00	3500,00	0,00	85000,00

Table 3.3.3 What will be your library's spending on eBooks intended primarily for children in 2016 (anticipated)? (All figures in $ US) Broken out by Size of full time equivalent library staff

Size of full time equivalent library staff	Mean	Median	Minimum	Maximum
1 or less	58,33	0,00	0,00	700,00
1+ -2.8	219,23	0,00	0,00	2000,00
2.8+ -6	420,00	225,00	0,00	2000,00
More than 6	10433,33	4500,00	500,00	85000,00

Table 3.3.4 What will be your library's spending on eBooks intended primarily for children in 2016 (anticipated)? (All figures in $ US) Broken out by Spending on print books ($)

Spending on print books ($)	Mean	Median	Minimum	Maximum
Less than 4500	350,00	0,00	0,00	5000,00
4500-14000	156,67	0,00	0,00	750,00
14000-30000	500,00	100,00	0,00	2000,00
More than 30000	10016,67	3500,00	0,00	85000,00

PRINT BOOK CULLING DECISION MAKING

What factors does the library take into account when it makes print book culling decisions? Broken out by Population of Library Service Area

Less than 3000
1) condition, last circulation date
2) Condition, whether the item is still relevant and in-demand, whether we have multiple copies or other books on the subject, how long it has been since last circulated, and sadly, if the cover is attractive. Patrons, children especially, will not check out a book with an old, dated cover.
3) age, condition, checkouts
4) age, condition, is it still being used
5) When it was last checked out, one shot only author, condition, currency of information.
6) Condition, usage, copyright dates, interest level of patrons
7) age , condition, demand
8) Age and lack of circulation
9) Series, Request, Best Seller List, Educational
10) need, price, space
11) Who reads them and will someone read them.
12) How often it was circulated in a specific time frame, & how outdated/ugly/dirty, or just plain M.U.S.T.Y. it is!
13) How many times it has been checked out. The shape the book is in. Author. Age.
14) Copy right date, condition of book, circulation, whether or not it is a memorial book.
15) Number of check outs condition of books publication date
16) public wishes

3000+ -7000
1) Condition, use, relevancy
2) condition, age, circulation, content (classics are kept even if not circulation much)
3) How old the book is, how many times it has been checked out
4) Space available and age
5) Popularity of book, cost, and long term usefulness
6) If the book is damaged and in a condition that is unhealthy to circulate to the public it is weeded.
7) We are entirely a local history and family history research library so weed very little. If something revised or something totally outdated.
8) publication date, circulation numbers
9) Condition of materials, circulation uses, out-of-date materials, patron interest
10) use in the last 5 years; shape the material is in
11) Condition of book and contents (misinformation).
12) Circulation, relevance, condition of the book, cost to replace, and possible reclassification to another area.

13) condition, relevance, use - all the usual
14) Number of eBooks being checked-out from consortia collection.
15) Popular titles and subjects needed

7000-19000

1) Age of content, circulation of title, popularity of author, and condition.
2) relevancy, condition of the book, currency
3) circulation, uniqueness, wear
4) Date of last check-out, age of book, book condition
5) check outs in 5 years, classic rating, generic appeal
6) subject popularity, author, reviews
7) Circulation, condition, age
8) Age, condition, popularity
9) We use TSLAC CREW manual
10) Circulation activity for book; attractiveness (lack of)
11) Use and condition
12) Depending on the funds available
13) Age, usage, condition
14) Content, condition, circulation statistics
15) If the book has circulated. If the book is current. If there is room on the shelves!

More than 19000

1) Popularity, Authoritativeness, Current, Relevancy, Physical Condition
2) Age of material, last circulation date, and condition.
3) condition, relevancy and accuracy, usage
4) Popularity of author, award winners, geographic authors
5) Frequency of previous use, better books now available, timeliness, condition
6) The library considers the condition of the book, the use of the book. Any book that has not circulated in 5 years is removed from the collection, unless it is a classic and is in good shape. If the book has poor circulation and is over 3 years old (ex: 3 years old and only circulated 2 times in its first year) it is weeded from the collection.
7) Circulation, condition, popularity of author, part of a series or no, digital availability
8) Relevance, condition, is there something better now to cover that topic, age, non-use
9) Standard weeding decisions as defined by CREW
10) If not circulated in 2 years, for the most part, item is removed. Items with heavy circulations are evaluated at every 40 or 100 circs depending on the collection.
11) relevance, timeliness, dated material, condition, number of titles in stock, popularity of the subject/author,
12) condition, check outs
13) Circulation, use of collection (history, business, car repair, biog, etc.)
14) If we remove a book in print it is because it is no longer circulating.
15) age and condition of materials and circulation numbers
16) copyright age, condition of book, circulation

PRINT BOOK COLLECTION VOLUME

Table 4 What is the total number of volumes in your library's print book collection for each of the following years:

Table 4.1.1 What was the total number of volumes in your library's print book collection 2014?

	Mean	Median	Minimum	Maximum
Entire sample	58325,17	21538,50	0,00	660000,00

Table 4.1.2 What was the total number of volumes in your library's print book collection 2014? Broken out by Population of Library Service Area

Population of Library Service Area	Mean	Median	Minimum	Maximum
Less than 3000	9306,00	10000,00	0,00	21250,00
3000+ -7000	20940,73	19072,00	8000,00	53000,00
7000-19000	29079,71	26242,00	4000,00	60000,00
More than 19000	164918,31	54018,00	27000,00	660000,00

Table 4.1.3 What was the total number of volumes in your library's print book collection 2014? Broken out by Size of full time equivalent library staff

Size of full time equivalent library staff	Mean	Median	Minimum	Maximum
1 or less	10260,11	10000,00	0,00	27000,00
1+ -2.8	20793,00	18786,00	4000,00	53000,00
2.8+ -6	30299,21	26242,00	13000,00	54036,00
More than 6	165070,19	55000,00	30000,00	660000,00

Public Library Plans for the Book Collection

Table 4.1.4 What was the total number of volumes in your library's print book collection 2014? Broken out by Spending on print books ($)

Spending on print books ($)	Mean	Median	Minimum	Maximum
Less than 4500	11388,07	9308,50	358,00	50000,00
4500-14000	19966,50	18864,50	0,00	53000,00
14000-30000	29069,13	26000,00	12000,00	54036,00
More than 30000	172305,07	60000,00	30000,00	660000,00

Table 4.2.1 What is the total number of volumes in your library's print book collection 2015?

	Mean	Median	Minimum	Maximum
Entire sample	59399,00	22408,50	420,00	645000,00

Table 4.2.2 What is the total number of volumes in your library's print book collection 2015? Broken out by Population of Library Service Area

Population of Library Service Area	Mean	Median	Minimum	Maximum
Less than 3000	10447,60	10500,00	420,00	21817,00
3000+ -7000	21437,33	18692,00	8000,00	56000,00
7000-19000	29804,93	27500,00	5000,00	58000,00
More than 19000	166774,81	54900,50	18000,00	645000,00

Table 4.2.3 What is the total number of volumes in your library's print book collection 2015? Broken out by Size of full time equivalent library staff

Size of full time equivalent library staff	Mean	Median	Minimum	Maximum
1 or less	10666,50	9750,00	420,00	21817,00
1+ -2.8	21578,92	18296,00	5000,00	56000,00
2.8+ -6	30335,79	27500,00	13000,00	54000,00
More than 6	168018,44	56900,50	33000,00	645000,00

Public Library Plans for the Book Collection

Table 4.2.4 What is the total number of volumes in your library's print book collection 2015? Broken out by Spending on print books ($)

Spending on print books ($)	Mean	Median	Minimum	Maximum
Less than 4500	11224,43	8500,00	420,00	50000,00
4500-14000	20950,31	18346,00	5000,00	56000,00
14000-30000	29213,20	26000,00	13000,00	54000,00
More than 30000	175559,67	58000,00	33000,00	645000,00

Table 4.3.1 What will be the total number of volumes in your library's print book collection2016 (anticipated)?

	Mean	Median	Minimum	Maximum
Entire sample	60460,00	23250,00	450,00	700000,00

Table 4.3.2 What will be the total number of volumes in your library's print book collection2016 (anticipated)? Broken out by Population of Library Service Area

Population of Library Service Area	Mean	Median	Minimum	Maximum
Less than 3000	9226,67	9000,00	450,00	22150,00
3000+ -7000	22066,67	19000,00	8000,00	59000,00
7000-19000	30357,14	29000,00	5000,00	55000,00
More than 19000	170825,00	54600,00	22000,00	700000,00

Table 4.3.3 What will be the total number of volumes in your library's print book collection2016 (anticipated)? Broken out by Size of full time equivalent library staff

Size of full time equivalent library staff	Mean	Median	Minimum	Maximum
1 or less	10077,78	9500,00	450,00	22150,00
1+ -2.8	22208,33	18500,00	5000,00	59000,00
2.8+ -6	30321,43	29000,00	13000,00	54000,00
More than 6	172200,00	55100,00	40000,00	700000,00

Public Library Plans for the Book Collection

Table 4.3.4 What will be the total number of volumes in your library's print book collection2016 (anticipated)? Broken out by Spending on print books ($)

Spending on print books ($)	Mean	Median	Minimum	Maximum
Less than 4500	11321,43	8750,00	450,00	50000,00
4500-14000	20368,75	18500,00	1900,00	59000,00
14000-30000	29733,33	26000,00	13000,00	54000,00
More than 30000	179813,33	55200,00	36000,00	700000,00

In which areas has the library been most aggressive in eliminating print titles and why in these areas? Broken out by Population of Library Service Area

Less than 3000

1) children's, as they were dated and in poor quality
2) Adult non-fiction. Demand is dwindling, non-fiction books are increasing in price, and the 900's are the only area that seem to still be circulating well.
3) adult, no room
4) romance & thrillers (paperbacks) - get bestsellers sent automatically and shelf room is limited
5) Nonfiction, reference, reasons include lack of use, space considerations.
6) Adult fiction-age of book and lack of circulation Science, medical, legal, test guides-age of book and the information it contains
7) no certain area
8) Teen age because they do not come in the library
9) All areas, check for age and series and check-out.
10) I usually do most of my book weeding in the adult section, I am very limited on space in my library. I hate to get rid of a children book unless it's in really bad shape. I can see which adult books aren't being read a lot and I can use the space for a book that more people want to read.
11) Fiction - most of our patrons want large print so regular print has been weeded.
12) Nonfiction, reference books, encyclopedias. Most of the information is available online.
13) Non-Fiction It had never been weeded. The age of the titles were old.
14) The 500's and 600's because so much of the information is very out of date.
15) Non-fiction titles. The need for updated and accurate information
16) we are not eliminating any

3000+ -7000

1) Adult Non-fiction/reference. Not enough usage to justify the cost of adding or retaining. Many people use the internet to research information.
2) Adult non-fiction, especially travel books, and biographies. Travel books are out-dated too soon. Folks who are traveling buy a current edition, and the other can use internet resources. Other non-fiction information is readily available and up-to-date on-line. Biographies tend to follow trends so I weed out ones that aren't being read.
3) In 2013 we did a very drastic culling on the entire library collection, probably most drastic in non-fiction. It is very hard to keep abreast in this area.
4) whatever areas need weeding most
5) Reference. Patrons use the internet.
6) Adult fiction because new publications are more frequently added and shelf space requires that we make room for the newer issues.
7) We have been eliminating non-Ohio duplicates in our lending library since many of the standard histories are online now.

8) none

9) Adult and Children's Fiction - very easy to gauge patron use and interest. Have to make room for new bestsellers.

10) Non-fiction- not use that we used to have.

11) Adult medical, fiction and reference. Youth non-fiction (all areas) and fiction. Eliminated because of non-use and misinformation.

12) We try to maintain our balance. We do not offer magazines or newspapers. We do not have the space.

13) YA & Juv fiction - because the kids aren't reading them

14) adult & children health/science, outdated information fiction titles of books worn out

15) N/a

7000-19000

1) Likely nonfiction, because the material gets dated faster.

2) no particular area - just outdated, unused items

3) Fiction. We have space for nonfiction, but space for fiction is very limited. Folks still have access through the 60+ library consortium we belong to. We have seamless requesting and a statewide delivery system for ILL.

4) Technology, reference. Rapid change in data and use of internet for information

5) encyclopedia volumes, information available on internet

6) nonfiction, frequent updates and less use by general public

7) Non-fiction -- in order to replace with more current titles. Both the adult and youth section. Also early readers as we have had donations of newer materials.

8) Non-Fiction. Out of Date. Mass Market books that are falling apart.

9) Our non-fiction collection has never been weeded!! This is what we are focusing on presently.

10) Adult non-fiction, to be sure to get rid of outdated material and items that have shown considerable lack of interest over a period of several years.

11) No specific areas. The library is full and we pretty much eliminate the same number that we purchase each year.

12) Fiction

13) Our community suffered a devastating flood in 2013. Our collection was reduced from 60,000 to less than 30,000 due to storage issues. All areas were aggressively weeded.

14) Nonfiction and particularly reference titles - they're outdated practically before cataloged. No point in purchasing printed materials when info is updated online daily.

15) Reference

More than 19000

1) Non-Fiction: We find much authoritative information found online and via databases.

2) All areas of nonfiction. They do not check out as much as our fiction does.

3) Reference because we have eBooks and databases to fill this need.

4) Non-fiction, picture books, any books/titles that are in poor condition.

5) Reference. So much ready reference is now being completed by computer.

6) We did a hard weed in adult fiction, children's picture books and Young Adult fiction last year. We also weeded Medical and Health information using the criteria that information (copyright date)

older than 8 years would be out-of-date information. We had many copyright dates from the 1970's and 1980's in our collection.

7) Reference, magazines, and large print collections. User preference is digital, cost per usage is cheaper digitally, currency of available materials is immediate with digital options

8) Reference--info is available online. Also, have moved most reference to circulating. Large Print--only limited appeal and hot title become cold very quickly.

9) Adult fiction - because there is a greater selection of e-books available through our current vendors

10) Non-fiction - usage has dropped most significantly here

11) Medicine, computers, law, teen materials -- the materials become dates quickly. Much of the information is able to be kept more up-to-date in digital format.

12) Reference books--Most times the most current info can be found on the internet. We keep basic information books on the shelves. For the most current data we use the net'

13) Cookbooks, business, duplicate fiction, pet care, personal growth.

14) Nonfiction titles that are out of date.

15) health (medical) and legal as these are changing all the time

16) Reference. The encyclopedias and such are not being utilized and are very outdated.

What has happened to your library's print book collection over the past five years? Is it larger than it was five years ago, in what areas has it grown? If it is smaller, in what areas has it diminished? Broken out by Population of Library Service Area

Less than 3000
1) Larger than 5 years ago, growth has been across the entire offering.
2) We've weeded out a lot of materials that weren't being read, or were old and worn. Our circulation has increased even though we have fewer volumes on the shelf. Less-crowded shelves are more attractive and patrons browse more.
3) its larger because there was an overweeding a few years ago that left the library lacking in books
4) More or less the same. Titles get added regularly and weeded thoroughly each three years when inventory is done.
5) Smaller due to aggressive weeding an out-of-date collection. Reference section, some non-fiction.
6) Larger than five years ago. Increased in easy children's and juvenile titles.
7) the same
8) It is smaller because we got rid of a lot of old donated books.
9) It is larger.
10) It has grown for sure, I always try to get a few books that correlate with the summer reading theme and I am always adding AR testing books in different levels for the kids to read and test on at school.
11) stayed about the same
12) The non-fiction has decreased, because I weeded reference materials that were from the 1960's, that hadn't left the shelf since then! Our adult fiction has increased, being in touch with our readers wants has been helpful.
13) Less. Weeded through some the books that have never been checked out & older copyrights.
14) It is larger in the last 5 years. Large print is the fastest growing section of the library.
15) The print book collection has remained about the same.
16) it is larger

3000+ -7000
1) It is smaller. Less non-fiction collection while fiction has stayed the same
2) It is smaller, mostly due to re-arranging the library. Adult non-fiction has been weeded the most.
3) It has grown. We have doubled our large print collection and probably our young adult section as well.
4) It is pretty much the same in the space available.
5) It is about the same.
6) The collections have grown in all areas. Print, audio, and eBook. Grant money, donations, author visits, library activities involve the public and they become aware of the many services the library provides. This involvement increases collection requests and enables the library to continue to encourage reading throughout the county.
7) Larger - most growth in local history section and in yearbook section (we have solicited them).
8) It is larger - adult fiction and non-fiction

9) About the same, but more interest in Adult Fiction and Children's Non-Fiction. Adult Non-Fiction and Reference have diminished as eBooks and Internet use have increased.

10) Smaller. Fiction collection remains the same. Large print collection has grown.

11) The fiction has gotten larger, and the non-fiction smaller, especially the reference.

12) It has grown, mostly through donations of local residents from five years ago.

13) about the same

14) Weed out. Christian fiction has grown, more demand. Adult Science fiction.

15) It remains the same

7000-19000

1) We did a major weed in 2014 bringing our collection from 33000 to approximately 26000. We weeded all areas.

2) larger - children's, adult fiction, young adult, local history, Native American, large print -- none has diminished

3) Collection has stayed pretty even due to space constraints.

4) Print collection has grown in large print, young adult, best sellers, children's

5) larger

6) It is much smaller. We have been weeding at a 3 to 1 ratio, 3 books out for every new one added. Our building was overrun with books no one used.

7) Larger

8) It is about the same size

9) Our collection has grown in our children's area, large print and adult fiction books. Collection is smaller in the non-fiction area.

10) Smaller. Has grown in Adult Fiction, Young Adult Fiction; has diminished in non-fiction.

11) It is slightly larger since 2011 when we took on additional space in the basement.

12) The same as years before.

13) Our patrons are very aware that the collection is much smaller than before the flood and looks forward to us being in a position to rebuild. Currently the collection has new titles however the depth of the collection has been reduced.

14) It stays fairly consistent in size as there is only so many shelves available to house collections. However, the individual collections have shifted over time - less nonfiction titles, reference is cut to 1/3 of titles but more in large print fiction, paperbacks and Christian fiction.

15) Reference has decreased

More than 19000

1) Smaller. Non-Fiction. Some genres such as westerns are no longer popular.

2) It has diminished. It has especially gotten smaller in nonfiction and fiction paperbacks such as Romance, Mystery, etc...

3) Our print collection is slightly smaller than it was five years ago, but mostly because we are lowering shelves and removing some shelving units to create more community space.

4) It continues to stay popular, less mass market paperback checkouts. It's about the same size just more current. Non-fiction not as popular as once was.

5) Due to financial constraints, it remains quite steady, except for the children's and YA collections which have grown enormously, thanks to a donor (children's book editor) of brand new books.

6) The collection is smaller because of the hard weeding we did. The area that has grown is large print books, children's books, and Young Adult books.

7) Smaller everywhere. Primarily in areas noted above; but smaller everywhere.

8) Collection continues to grow. Mostly growing in children's & YA collections. (Our population has tripled in the last 10 years)

9) We are a zero growth library, so we are at capacity, and weed to maintain the level we are at.

10) Increased by 10,000 items

11) It is slightly larger and not anticipated to continue to grow. We do collect more copies of bestsellers; however the primary reason that is has grown is because we added a branch to our system

12) We have grown in the large print area as we have an aging population and we have worked to develop a small Spanish collection.

13) Smaller. Weeded lots of go-to nonfiction books (people get the info online).

14) It has grown, but due to limitations of space we reduced collection size to make it easier to browse. Print circulation is up 14% this year.

15) It remains about the same.

16) Print is smaller as a result of a massive weeding of outdated nonfiction items. Some of the nonfiction areas are not being utilized and will not be replaced because the most updated information can be found online. Fiction is still my most utilized area so it will continue to grow.

In your view what will happen to your library's print book collection over the next five years? Will it become larger or smaller? If so, what areas will be most affected and why? Will spending remain the same? Increase or decrease? Broken out by Population of Library Service Area

Less than 3000

1) Smaller as we purchase less nonfiction. Spending will probably be around the same, increasing only as costs increase.

2) It will probably shrink a bit but should remain relatively stable. With a small library of limited size, we need to constantly be removing older books and adding newer titles as demand changes, or we'd be out of room in a few months. We're cutting back spending on most adult non-fiction titles unless patrons ask for them, and we've also seen a drop in e-book demand; many patrons have gone back to regular books. Others who are using e-books seem to prefer to purchase them rather than borrow them. Spending will probably decrease overall in future years as our city starts cutting budgets. With much more demand on libraries recently as community centers and sources for free internet/Wi-Fi, we've had to funnel more of our funding into areas other than books. Sadly, small libraries, especially, are being asked to add more and more services with less and less money, so something has to give.

3) larger, spending will hopefully be the same

4) We have a fair number of older clientele who are not comfortable with electronic resources. As they age, I expect that numbers will be affected but do not see change happening for a few years

5) Decrease in size, will not buy some of the more contemporary fiction. Spending will probably stay the same, as book costs continue to rise.

6) Print collection will probably become smaller, especially in the fiction areas. Spending for print materials will probably decrease.

7) the same

8) Probably stay the same. We have no purchase budget so we just use donated books.

9) About the same as now.

10) I wish it could become larger, but I have the space issue that I know will not be changing anytime soon. I believe that things will stay the same, just books that are keeping up with the trends for the readers.

11) It will remain the same, large print and children's will increase. Adult reg. print and junior books will decrease due to lack of use.

12) I will continue to refurnish the non-fiction/reference collection with materials that are more of what our readers want, slow process, as they are a bit more pricey than Fiction. Our children's collection needs more materials, so will weed, and re-fill, also purchase more reader levels. I see our collection staying about the same #'s, with an increase to our "other" collections growing through donations.., cake pans, puzzles, games (board & electronic). Possibly tablets to loan out, also. If budget remains the same or increases, we will not decrease our materials budget.

13) Remain about the same in numbers. Starting to buy more local story & history books. Trying to keep the collection fresh.

14) I think the print book collection will continue to increase over the next 5 years. Most of my patrons want to have a book in their hand to read. If anything spending will decrease as the town sees areas other than the library as ways to use their money.

15) This is difficult to gage. A lot depends on what the library patrons want.

16) it will become larger

3000+ -7000

1) I think overall size will remain constant, but non-fiction will continue to shrink for a while, but DVDs, audio and e-books will continue to grow

2) I think the adult collection will stay about the same size - basically buy one, weed one philosophy. The teen area is badly in need of more books and that is where dollars will be spent. Spending over all will stay about the same.

3) We will continue to increase our print collection. It is by far more popular even among our patrons who utilize the eBook section.

4) It will probably be about the same. Hopefully more funds will be available, as they have been significantly cut in the past two years.

5) Probably will remain the same.

6) I hope the collections and spending will increase in all areas! Increasing literacy programs and activities for all ages; creating an atmosphere of life-long learning, encouraging participation in library events, and introducing new authors and ideas is important for a community's growth.

7) Larger. Spending will remain same although we are currently seeking funding for expansion of our African America genealogy collection.

8) The print collection will continue to grow in all areas of the library's collection. Spending will continue to increase.

9) I hope to maintain current numbers in print, but different collections will change. More Adult and Children's Fiction. I don't foresee a change in overall budget amount, just shifting more to eBooks and eReference.

10) Someone smaller depending on the demand and who are our users. Homeschoolers have put us back in the non-fiction buying area.

11) The print will continue to shrink, especially in the medical and nonfiction areas where quality information is readily available in online databases.

12) We are at capacity with print material. We have very limited seating. We would like to grow digitally. Spending will remain the same.

13) become small, mostly in fiction

14) Probably remain the same. However, we do expect to increase in our eBook collection.

15) It should remain the same. If the library sees a want for eBooks we will add titles to the already printed title.

7000-19000

1) We hope to replace a lot of the deleted material, to bring our collection available back up. However, some of those titles will definitely be eBooks. We tend to spend approximately 2-5% of our budget on eBook titles each year.

2) I think it will stay about the same and spending will probably stay about the same.

3) Print book collection will remain the same as will spending.

4) Spending will be static due to city budget constraints. Collection will focus on culling older non-fiction and increasing children and young adult new genres

5) Static or diminish in reference sections - internet resources. Spending level or increase

6) We hope to maintain or continue to shrink the collection as more people switch to eBooks and we are able to adapt our space for a more modern library.

7) If we are able to start using e-books, it will become smaller. Otherwise, it will remain more or less the same size.

8) It will stay about the same.

9) Most likely, our collection will stay close to the same.

10) Collection will likely stay the same, and spending may decrease some.

11) I don't expect much change. Circulation is down mostly for the romance collections and it was never a large part of our collection. We borrow less these from other libraries in our system. Our only change has been to be more active in taking recommendations from our patrons for item purchases.

12) Larger

13) The collection will grow but it will be a balancing process to insure that eBook and print readers have titles available to them.

14) Would expect overall print to diminish over time. Not sure if spending will remain the same or decrease dependent on cost of print vs. eBook titles. Will continue to increase digital spending by 5%/year, probably at the expense of print materials.

15) about the same

More than 19000

1) Our print collection will probably be a bit smaller, based on format needs of our patrons. We are increasing our Playaway budget as this is a very popular format. We also have a healthy book on CD budget.

2) I think our print collection will continue to become smaller. Our media items have been increasing in circulation as well as online resources. I think we will continue to weed out more nonfiction as resources become available on the web. I think the spending will continue to decrease.

3) It will grow slightly because we are building three new larger buildings.

4) Think it will stay the same but just be more current. Also depends on space.

5) Hopefully, spending will increase and the collection will grow somewhat.

6) The plans are to weed informational materials hard soon. This will decrease the size of the collection. Materials will be reviewed and added as needed. The library budget for books will remain steady with an increase every two years if I can get it approved.

7) Continue to decrease. Spending is likely to remain fairly consistent as budgets are not changing, and as we see how patrons respond/request.

8) I believe it will continue to grow but mostly in the reading-for-entertainment areas. We are continuously increasing our children's & YA collections. I believe spending will remain pretty steady in the future.

9) Will stay the same size - since we are zero growth.

10) It will become smaller. Partly due to having a good data mining product like Collection HQ to assist in weeding and partly due to move toward electronic formats

Public Library Plans for the Book Collection

11) Unless additional branches are added, we expect the print collection to begin to contract within the next five years. We expect the reduction to effect the entire collection -- adult more than juvenile materials. We expect overall collection spending to increase slightly, but the amount spent on print will decrease in favor of AV and digital.

12) Both of the above areas will continue to grow. I can see that the non-fiction are will decrease as people use the internet for more of that info

13) Slightly smaller. We have lots of readers who love books per se, not eBooks. Children's pic bks still very much used. Nonfiction, except the blockbusters like Dead Wake or Boys in the Boat, will decrease.

14) Spending for print will increase because we see that eBooks are like audiobooks, they have their place but they are not a replacement for print.

15) It will probably remain about the same but this may change depending on the demand

16) The fiction will continue to be weeded of outdated and musty books and will replace with fresh new books. The nonfiction is changing and some areas will continue to be utilized and will grow, but some areas will be better off finding information on the internet because of the importance of having updated content.

PRINT BOOK CULLING STRATEGY

Table 5.1 Approximately what percentage of your print book collection did you cull in the past year?

	Mean	Median	Minimum	Maximum
Entire sample	12,36	8,00	1,00	100,00

Table 5.2 Approximately what percentage of your print book collection did you cull in the past year? Broken out by Population of Library Service Area

Population of Library Service Area	Mean	Median	Minimum	Maximum
Less than 3000	20,21	10,00	3,00	100,00
3000+ -7000	7,20	5,00	1,00	20,00
7000-19000	11,04	10,00	1,00	50,00
More than 19000	11,35	10,00	1,00	30,00

Table 5.3 Approximately what percentage of your print book collection did you cull in the past year? Broken out by Size of full time equivalent library staff

Size of full time equivalent library staff	Mean	Median	Minimum	Maximum
1 or less	19,39	10,00	3,00	100,00
1+ -2.8	6,88	5,00	1,00	20,00
2.8+ -6	7,50	5,50	1,00	20,00
More than 6	12,59	10,00	1,00	50,00

Table 5.4 Approximately what percentage of your print book collection did you cull in the past year? Broken out by Spending on print books ($)

Spending on print books ($)	Mean	Median	Minimum	Maximum
Less than 4500	20,43	10,00	3,00	100,00
4500-14000	7,73	5,00	1,00	30,00
14000-30000	8,97	10,00	1,00	20,00
More than 30000	12,95	10,00	1,00	50,00

If the library has changed its book acquisitions and/or book collection culling strategy over the past five years, or expects to change it soon, please describe these changes. Broken out by Population of Library Service Area

Less than 3000
1) no
2) We used to cull only books that were badly-damaged or hadn't circulated in 5 years. I now cull more frequently based on what interests and needs I see in our patrons. Some books that are 10 years old are still here, while others that are only a year or two old are gone if they haven't been read. Space is at a premium since we've had to remove some shelves to make space for more patron seating and computer areas, so titles need to be circulating frequently or they won't be here long.
3) none
4) Keep on weeding, cleaning up collection to make it look brighter and more appealing.
5) No changes.
6) no
7) No changes
8) Weeding out
9) na
10) Purchasing about the same just different areas.
11) We have not made any changes in our acquisitioning process, nor our weeding process, nor do we expect to anytime in the near future.
12) The library will buy best sellers & what we can in patron request.
13) I am using more purchase plan companies to increase the book acquisitions.
14) N/A

3000+ -7000
1) We began using the CREW method. Previously, non-fiction was not weeded unless the copyright was at least 10 years old and hadn't been checked out in 5 years.
2) We are in the process of building a new library. With more shelving (hopefully) we will be adding more books.
3) n/a
4) none expected
5) Hasn't changed.
6) Culling is done as needed. We do not have a specific 'culling time'. Generally we do an inventory each year and much culling is done at this time.
7) No plan to change.
8) no changes at this time
9) No major changes in weeding, but changes have been in budget for more Fiction and less Non-Fiction and Reference.

10) keeping with the 5 year rule
11) No changes anticipated.
12) We continue to use the CREW method.
13) We are more ruthless
14) Probably not much change, unless higher demand for eBooks.

7000-19000

1) no
2) no changes
3) More aggressive
4) review of reference section for unneeded purchases
5) With an entirely new administration and selection team our strategy has changed a great deal. It is difficult to put the strategy into words other than supply what our audience wants and remove what they don't.
6) n/a
7) No changes. We try to do one area of our collection each year.
8) No changes occurred nor anticipated; we use the CREW method and it works well for us.
9) No changes
10) No change
11) N/A

More than 19000

1) No change, but will keep an eye on user patterns and format availability.
2) We are using Collection HQ reports to more aggressively weed by setting parameters such as last time circulated.
3) We have not changed our strategies in these areas significantly.
4) No change
5) The library changed its strategy because of education of the library director. She obtained a Master's degree in Library and Information Studies. It changed her thought process about books, a book only is a book if it has a reader. It is important to keep fresh material on hand, I would not want to be treated by a Doctor that relied on 1970's medical information.
6) No change in methods.
7) We tend to weed aggressively. Not really changing anything.
8) We are weeding more aggressively, in order to maintain the collection size. We are also actively shifting to eBooks whenever possible.
9) Using Collection HQ we will continue to cull, but probably closer to 15% over the next three years
10) The library moved to an ongoing three year weeding schedule. The general rule of thumb is for every 6 new books added to the collection we expect to weed 5.
11) have not changed
12) Yes, more aggressive as we run out of space
13) No changes in strategy for now.

In what areas do you believe that the library will be most aggressive in culling print books in the future? In what areas or subjects do you believe that the library is likely to increase spending on print books? Broken out by Population of Library Service Area

Less than 3000

1) Cull-nonfiction spending-middle teen and locally authored fiction.
2) We are culling non-fiction aggressively as demand wanes; children's books less so than adult, although demand for kids' non-fiction is less in many areas as well. Audio books are also falling out of favor. Most of our additional print spending will be on large print books-- this area is by far our fastest- growing demand area.
3) kids section
4) not drastically
5) Nonfiction, reference. Children's authors who are no longer read.
6) More aggressive in culling adult fiction. May increase spending in the non-fiction areas.
7) no
8) Old tatty children's books
9) All ages
10) na
11) Increase in Christian Fiction and lg. print adult, and the children's 0 to 7 area.
12) I started 8 years ago, & that was when aggression was the word of the day when we weeded. Now, our collection is at a point where our non-fiction (mostly adult) collection needs replenishing with books that our patrons want to see. Gardening, DIY home projects, self-help (grief & diet & anxiety issues), cookbooks, History, and True Crime.
13) Need to look at fiction this next year. Shelves are getting full.
14) Nonfiction books will be culled as they become out of date. Large print fiction spending will increase.
15) The library will try to balance weeding both fiction and nonfiction books in both the adult and children's area. The type of patron and their interests who determine who print materials are added to the library.
16) We are moving to a new building that is much bigger. I will be adding more self-help, cookbooks and how to books

3000+ -7000

1) We will continue to be aggressive in the non-fiction culling. We are becoming a more patron-demand based library, so we will grow in the areas our community asks.
2) Adult non-fiction and Adult fiction. We will be increasing spending on young adult books but we will also be weeding that area.
3) culling - non-fiction increasing spending in: juvenile fiction, adult fiction
4) remain the same
5) Non-fiction. People use on-line sources for more of their information.
6) Probably in the adult and children's fiction areas. These areas will also show increase as well as the nonfiction sections. Audio for adults will probably continue to increase.

Public Library Plans for the Book Collection

7) Sorry, we are such a specialty library that it isn't fitting your survey. Do not plan to change culling percentage, nor plan to increase print book expenditures.
8) Increase spending will continue in all areas of the print material.
9) Fiction is always the most aggressive for Adult and Children's materials. I don't see much increase in spending on print books of any kind.
10) non-fiction, juvenile fiction,
11) Areas that demand current info (medical, legal, political, science) will be weeded. I am not looking for an increase in spending on print books.
12) We would like to spend more in Non-fiction areas.
13) history, art for increased spending
14) Probably biography. Fiction titles.
15) Children's

7000-19000
1) Same as previous.
2) outdated medical books cannot hope to increase, but to at least stay the same
3) See previous
4) Reference. STEM
5) Our children's books will be heavily purchased in the next several years to replace an aged and neglected collection
6) Culling-mass-market and non-fiction Increase spending - none
7) After the non-fiction collection the adult fiction books will be culled.
8) Future culling will be most aggressive in non-fiction (adult and children's levels) and juvenile fiction chapter books. Non-fiction (adult) will probably see an increase in spending on print books.
9) I purchase less medical and reference books.
10) Both in fiction and the non-fiction collections. Especially in the 600 medical
11) Fiction and popular nonfiction are still really important to our population. EBooks are not necessarily replacing print but augmenting in another format.
12) We will continue to aggressively cull nonfiction materials. Other collections will be culled on a rotating basis.
13) Reference

More than 19000
1) Non-Fiction areas will be aggressive. We will continue a healthy print easy reader/picture book collection as we are encouraging literacy development and reading to children. We will continue to purchase best sellers and books in demand.
2) I think nonfiction will continue to be cut for the most part. Our customers seem to enjoy new fiction and children's books.
3) We won't increase spending on print, except to freshen up certain areas of the collection. For example, our picture books have an average turnover of 14 times per year. We will spend to replace the items that are in poor condition due to high use. We do these projects as needed.
4) Areas that don't circulate and books that are in bad condition.
5) I don't really know about any aggressive culling--none planned. If we increase spending, fiction first.

Public Library Plans for the Book Collection

6) I plan to weed the informational books in the future. I will increase spending in fiction, carefully selected informational books for all ages.

7) I can't see any area where spending on print will increase, it will likely only remain consistent on new release, best sellers. We consistently cull the collection as a standard practice, so there is no one area of focus.

8) Items not circulating.

9) Yes

10) Non-fiction primarily, but all collections are in need. Probably increase spending on children's and fiction

11) Medicine, law, computers. I don't believe we will increase spending on print.

12) culling non-fiction and increase in Spanish (both adult and children's) and large print

13) More copies of literary fiction, best sellers, novels that book groups want. Fewer copies of standard nonfiction, except blockbusters and big authors.

14) We cull old out of date books.

15) Medical, Legal   Teen, Graphic Novels, Nonfiction

16) On an ongoing basis, I am culling more and more adult nonfiction - 600, 800 and the whole YA nonfiction section for the reasons of nonuse or outdated information. I will increase spending on relevant adult nonfiction 600, 200. Adult, teen and juvenile fiction print will see increased spending along with juvenile nonfiction.

SPACE ISSUES

Table 6.1 If the library has reduced the size of its book collection in recent years, has this led to an increase in space that the library can use for other purposes?

	No Answer	Yes	No
Entire sample	6,45%	33,87%	59,68%

Table 6.2 If the library has reduced the size of its book collection in recent years, has this led to an increase in space that the library can use for other purposes? Broken out by Population of Library Service Area

Population of Library Service Area	No Answer	Yes	No
Less than 3000	0,00%	43,75%	56,25%
3000+ -7000	13,33%	33,33%	53,33%
7000-19000	13,33%	13,33%	73,33%
More than 19000	0,00%	43,75%	56,25%

Table 6.3 If the library has reduced the size of its book collection in recent years, has this led to an increase in space that the library can use for other purposes? Broken out by Size of full time equivalent library staff

Size of full time equivalent library staff	No Answer	Yes	No
1 or less	0,00%	42,11%	57,89%
1+ -2.8	23,08%	15,38%	61,54%
2.8+ -6	7,14%	28,57%	64,29%
More than 6	0,00%	43,75%	56,25%

Table 6.4 If the library has reduced the size of its book collection in recent years, has this led to an increase in space that the library can use for other purposes? Broken out by Spending on print books ($)

Spending on print books ($)	No Answer	Yes	No
Less than 4500	0,00%	37,50%	62,50%
4500-14000	18,75%	43,75%	37,50%
14000-30000	6,67%	6,67%	86,67%
More than 30000	0,00%	46,67%	53,33%

If space has been freed-up over the past five years how much space and how is this space now being deployed? Broken out by Population of Library Service Area

Less than 3000

1) increased computer area and additional shelving area for rearranging current holdings
2) Additional seating for patrons, additional space for computer areas.
3) More meeting space, more space for children to play with games and puzzles.
4) No freed-up space.
5) To better arrange books so they are more appealing
6) 200 ft. maybe, used for referencing history, entertainment & classic books.
7) We are only 635 sq. ft. We utilized the "New Releases & purchases" bookcase to start a movie (DVD & Blu-ray) collection. Our community has no rental options for movies. We now have over 300 movies for all ages! This also gave us some room for a couple of chairs and a round table without losing our Handicap Accessible space.
8) The freed up space is being used for a meeting place.
9) Book shelf space is used to highlight authors and titles and is also used to display various items of interest.
10) What we have weeded was to make room for newer books.

3000+ -7000

1) We increased the space for teens and added furnishings that appeal to them. We were also able to add some smaller study areas and areas for use of personal electronic devices
2) We now have a small sitting area with a table. We lost about two 72" x 144" double sided shelving ranges when we re-arranged. But the library looks wonderful now!
3) additional room added for audio books
4) n/a
5) N/A
6) use for display collections
7) No free space.
8) more seating,
9) N/A
10) The space is now being used for computer access

7000-19000

1) n/a
2) Small space now being used for individual reading and BYOD areas
3) Any space gained used for facings, display.
4) We have created sitting and group study areas, added two research sections and created a storytime zone as well as creating dedicated spaces for computers, laptops and printing.
5) We had an expansion that doubled our space and enabled us to hold the collection we have comfortably and have space for programs

6) Any space freed up is used to shelve newer books. We continue to purchase (monthly) best-sellers and popular authors/series in both fiction and non-fiction.

7) n/a

8) it is reused for the new acquisitions

9) We did not have additional space as the library was housed in temporary quarters. Our shelves were just as full but fewer shelves too! Libraries need additional

10) More than 19000

11) We are using additional shelving for display and shelf-space for books on CD. This year we are shifting non-fiction to add additional shelf space for Playaways. We weeded older LP, Westerns and Science Fiction to expand our YA or Teen space. Our biographies were moved to another part of the library, next to our magazines and newspapers.

12) We put in a maker space and allowed for more room between collections for customer convenience.

13) We have freed up some community meeting space by reducing collections. We plan to have much more community space in our new larger buildings. Though the buildings are twice as large as the old buildings, the collections will only be 20% larger. Seating and meeting space is the goal.

14) Not being used.

15) N/A

16) The space that was obtained from the major weed allows books not to be placed on the top and bottom shelf unless necessary. This allows the patrons to easily reach books.

17) Our shelves were very overcrowded, even dramatic culling has really just improved shelving appearance; we are not taking out shelves yet (yet!).

18) haven't reduced

19) na

20) additional study and meeting areas for increase programming

21) We cut almost all our 90" stacks down to 36" or 44" high, leaving lots of visual display room. Nonfiction is an open area, great for browsing. Added study rooms w/ glass walls, extra meeting rooms, big Reading Room for newspapers/mags.

22) Only shelf space to increase browsing - it was too crowded.

23) Yes space has been freed up for other activities, programs, technology

24) I am using the space vacated by Reference for an Espanol section. In the teen section I will use the space vacated by nonfiction to hold Graphic novels.

OPINION OF LIBRARY PATRONS ON PRINT VS. DIGITAL

Table 7.1 Has the library surveyed its patrons on their preferences for print vs. digital resources as a prelude to decision making on reducing the size of book collections?

	No Answer	Yes	No
Entire sample	0,00%	27,42%	72,58%

Table 7.2 Has the library surveyed its patrons on their preferences for print vs. digital resources as a prelude to decision making on reducing the size of book collections? Broken out by Population of Library Service Area

Population of Library Service Area	Yes	No
Less than 3000	25,00%	75,00%
3000+ -7000	26,67%	73,33%
7000-19000	26,67%	73,33%
More than 19000	31,25%	68,75%

Table 7.3 Has the library surveyed its patrons on their preferences for print vs. digital resources as a prelude to decision making on reducing the size of book collections? Broken out by Size of full time equivalent library staff

Size of full time equivalent library staff	Yes	No
1 or less	26,32%	73,68%
1+ -2.8	23,08%	76,92%
2.8+ -6	28,57%	71,43%
More than 6	31,25%	68,75%

Table 7.4 Has the library surveyed its patrons on their preferences for print vs. digital resources as a prelude to decision making on reducing the size of book collections? Broken out by Spending on print books ($)

Spending on print books ($)	Yes	No
Less than 4500	12,50%	87,50%
4500-14000	50,00%	50,00%
14000-30000	6,67%	93,33%
More than 30000	40,00%	60,00%

Table 8.1 Which phrase would you say best describes your Friends of the Library organization's opinion about using library resources for increasing spending on print books or eBooks

	No Answer	Tend to be more supportive of eBooks	Tend to be more supportive of Print Books	Don't really take a position on the issue
Entire sample	6,45%	1,61%	20,97%	70,97%

Table 8.2 Which phrase would you say best describes your Friends of the Library organization's opinion about using library resources for increasing spending on print books or eBooks Broken out by Population of Library Service Area

Population of Library Service Area	No Answer	Tend to be more supportive of eBooks	Tend to be more supportive of Print Books	Don't really take a position on the issue
Less than 3000	6,25%	0,00%	25,00%	68,75%
3000+ -7000	13,33%	0,00%	13,33%	73,33%
7000-19000	0,00%	0,00%	20,00%	80,00%
More than 19000	6,25%	6,25%	25,00%	62,50%

Table 8.3 Which phrase would you say best describes your Friends of the Library organization's opinion about using library resources for increasing spending on print books or eBooks Broken out by Size of full time equivalent library staff

Size of full time equivalent library staff	No Answer	Tend to be more supportive of eBooks	Tend to be more supportive of Print Books	Don't really take a position on the issue
1 or less	10,53%	0,00%	21,05%	68,42%
1+ -2.8	7,69%	0,00%	7,69%	84,62%
2.8+ -6	0,00%	0,00%	28,57%	71,43%

More than 6	6,25%	6,25%	25,00%	62,50%

Table 8.4 Which phrase would you say best describes your Friends of the Library organization's opinion about using library resources for increasing spending on print books or eBooks Broken out by Spending on print books ($)

Spending on print books ($)	No Answer	Tend to be more supportive of eBooks	Tend to be more supportive of Print Books	Don't really take a position on the issue
Less than 4500	6,25%	0,00%	18,75%	75,00%
4500-14000	12,50%	0,00%	31,25%	56,25%
14000-30000	0,00%	0,00%	20,00%	80,00%
More than 30000	6,67%	6,67%	13,33%	73,33%

Table 9.1 In your view local school districts in the library's service area tend to want the library to:

	No Answer	Prioritize eBooks in library purchasing decisions	Prioritize Print Books in library purchasing decisions	Don't seem to have a preference	Impact on Use of Storage Space
Entire sample	1,61%	3,23%	17,74%	77,42%	0,00%

Table 9.2 In your view local school districts in the library's service area tend to want the library to: Broken out by Population of Library Service Area

Population of Library Service Area	No Answer	Prioritize eBooks in library purchasing decisions	Prioritize Print Books in library purchasing decisions	Don't seem to have a preference	Impact on Use of Storage Space
Less than 3000	0,00%	6,25%	12,50%	81,25%	0,00%
3000+ -7000	6,67%	0,00%	20,00%	73,33%	0,00%
7000-19000	0,00%	0,00%	20,00%	80,00%	0,00%
More than 19000	0,00%	6,25%	18,75%	75,00%	0,00%

Table 9.3 In your view local school districts in the library's service area tend to want the library to: Broken out by Size of full time equivalent library staff

Size of full time equivalent library staff	No Answer	Prioritize eBooks in library purchasing decisions	Prioritize Print Books in library purchasing decisions	Don't seem to have a preference	Impact on Use of Storage Space
1 or less	5,26%	5,26%	10,53%	78,95%	0,00%
1+ -2.8	0,00%	0,00%	23,08%	76,92%	0,00%
2.8+ -6	0,00%	0,00%	14,29%	85,71%	0,00%
More than 6	0,00%	6,25%	25,00%	68,75%	0,00%

Table 9.4 In your view local school districts in the library's service area tend to want the library to: Broken out by Spending on print books ($)

Spending on print books ($)	No Answer	Prioritize eBooks in library purchasing decisions	Prioritize Print Books in library purchasing decisions	Don't seem to have a preference	Impact on Use of Storage Space
Less than 4500	6,25%	6,25%	12,50%	75,00%	0,00%
4500-14000	0,00%	0,00%	18,75%	81,25%	0,00%
14000-30000	0,00%	0,00%	13,33%	86,67%	0,00%
More than 30000	0,00%	6,67%	26,67%	66,67%	0,00%

CULLED MATERIALS HANDLING

Table 10.1 Does the library use offsite storage for books, journals and other printed materials?

	No Answer	Yes	No
Entire sample	0,00%	4,84%	95,16%

Table 10.2 Does the library use offsite storage for books, journals and other printed materials? Broken out by Population of Library Service Area

Population of Library Service Area	Yes	No
Less than 3000	6,25%	93,75%
3000+ -7000	6,67%	93,33%
7000-19000	0,00%	100,00%
More than 19000	6,25%	93,75%

Table 10.3 Does the library use offsite storage for books, journals and other printed materials? Broken out by Size of full time equivalent library staff

Size of full time equivalent library staff	Yes	No
1 or less	5,26%	94,74%
1+ -2.8	0,00%	100,00%
2.8+ -6	7,14%	92,86%
More than 6	6,25%	93,75%

Table 10.4 Does the library use offsite storage for books, journals and other printed materials? Broken out by Spending on print books ($)

Spending on print books ($)	Yes	No
Less than 4500	6,25%	93,75%
4500-14000	6,25%	93,75%
14000-30000	0,00%	100,00%
More than 30000	6,67%	93,33%

Has the amount of space used for offsite storage increased or decreased in recent years and if so by how much? Also what has been the trend in storage costs? Broken out by Population of Library Service Area

Less than 3000
1) n/a
2) We do not have off-site storage; we have very little storage in the library, either. If we don't have room for it, we don't have it.
3) NA
4) N/A
5) No change
6) Our off-site storage consists of the attic of the community building. My storage needs have increased, along with the increase of operating hours & programming (there were no programs & was open 12 1/2 hrs week) 8 yrs. ago when I came on board. We have had so many books & arts & craft materials donated we needed a whole closet (library has none), & we store books & such materials in the attic. Some things are put into lockable totes & placed in the basement & put on wooden pallets, because the basement leaks. I have some elementary school materials that are in the basement that are 8 mm filmstrips with accompanying vinyl albums that are in basement in large locking totes. Hoping they last down there until I can find a way or place for them. No monetary cost to store, but has stirred some animosity from comm. org. that don't like sharing attic space with me!

3000+ -7000
7) N/A
8) N/A
9) n/a
10) n/a
11) N/A
12) No money in the budget for offsite storage.
13) N/A

7000-19000
1) NA
2) n/a
3) n/a
4) no storage
5) Not applicable.

More than 19000
1) We have moved all off-site storage of historic furnishings to our onsite-garage. We have no off-site storage for print materials.
2) No

3) Storage costs are up and it's hard to find adequate storage nearby. We plan to use offsite storage more to house seasonal collections that we don't want to warehouse on the shelves in our libraries.
4) N/A
5) N/A
6) na
7) NA
8) N/A

What kinds of data does your library use in making print materials culling decisions and how does each data set contribute to your decision making? Broken out by Population of Library Service Area

Less than 3000
1) n/a
2) Circulation statistics are most important. These let us see what is circulating, what isn't, and what authors/subjects are most popular.
3) Checkout records, physical condition of book, reviews of questionable materials, i.e., racism, viewpoint bias, space exploration, etc.
4) We use the CREW Method recommended by the Texas State Library and Archives Commission.
5) We keep classics and popular authors.
6) Book System
7) not checked out for 3 years
8) We use the CREW Method. Developed by the Texas State Library and Archives Commission in 1995. Specifically geared for Small and Medium-Sized Public Libraries. This involves using the "MUSTIE acronym. Misleading (and/or factually inaccurate), Ugly, Superseded, Trivial, Irrelevant, E=the material may be obtained expeditiously Elsewhere through ILL or otherwise.
9) Number of times the book has been checked out.
10) I don't use any kind of data to make culling decisions.
11) the crew manual
12) number of checkouts and condition of the book

3000+ -7000
1) We use the CREW manual for culling guidelines and then run circulation reports to see which titles need to be weeded due to non-use
2) Circulation stats. We look at the circulation and use that information to help make a decision. It is not the sole deciding factor.
3) none used
4) Checkouts, age of book.
5) CREW from the state library
6) We look at historical content and if book contains a lot of names.
7) stats are the main source of information for culling material
8) Condition of materials, circulation uses, out-of-date materials, patron interest
9) last check out; age of book; circulation numbers
10) Number of check-outs, age of book, date of last check-out. Is it part of a series? If a fiction book is at least 10 years old, and has not checked out in the last 5, it is a candidate for weeding.
11) Circulation reports from our system are a good place for us to start.
12) Collection HQ
13) Crew manual

Public Library Plans for the Book Collection

7000-19000

1) Publication year, and circulation statistics. We look at the relevance of the material based on the year. This has more of an effect when we are looking at non-fiction. We also look at when the last time a book was checked out was, and how many checkouts it's had in its lifetime. This helps us decide if it's something our patrons would miss if we took it off the shelf, or if we can make room for newer titles by culling it.

2) last date checked out and how many times checked out Both sets of data contribute the same to the item's relevancy to the community

3) The library is a member of the Maine Shared Collection Consortium which analyses collections looking for unique titles which will be retained for 15 years--all others are available for weeding.

4) NA

5) primarily, usage patterns

6) circulation, condition, uniqueness

7) How materials are being used, circulation, condition etc. Circulation numbers are the main data set used in making decisions

8) age and content

9) Circulation statistics over the past 5 years, aggressive culling in fiction. For non-fiction, we definitely look at whether the material is outdated and get rid of anything that is out of date; but we also consider replacing the material with new, updated items.

10) Circulation of the item. Last time circulated.

11) NA

12) How often the titles has been used; last use of the item; condition; availability within our regional consortium

13) Standard library rules for nonfiction, fiction and children's based on condition, content and circulation.

More than 19000

1) Circulation statistics from our automation system, Innovative.

2) Reports from Sirsi and Collection HQ.

3) We first use usage. Has the item checked out in the last 6 months? Is it older than 2 years and has fewer than a certain number of checkouts this year? Is it in poor condition? (Would you take that book to bed with you?) Is it out of date?

4) Circ frequency

5) We use our ILS to scan and read the circulation statistics. It also gives us the date the book was placed in circulation. It is not hard to let a book go that has been in the library 30 years and never been checked out. I think that would describe 1% of the books that left, most had not circulated in the last five years.

6) Circulation and condition are primary, popularity is secondary, and availability of ematerial is considered.

7) Usage, last use date---Tend to purchase items we know will circulate, don't spend as much on "iffy" items.

8) CREW manual recommendations, and ILS data about circulation.

9) Collection HQ is a robust product offers excellent stats for usage, age, etc. In addition giving access to marketing and collection tools such as finding what items on a topic during a specific publication time are high circulation in other libraries.

10) Copyright date, age of acquisition, number of copies, circulation history. For fiction circulation history and number of copies plays a larger role. For nonfiction copyright date is more important.

11) core collections, item usage, condition

12) Besides looking at circulation stats, our librarians know the collections and our community needs.

13) Circulation stats

14) Our Plan of Service

15) Usage reports, copyright age reports contribute greatly to my decision making.

Table 11.1 Approximately what percentage of your culled book collection is given away to schools, libraries, charitable agencies or other venues?

	Mean	Median	Minimum	Maximum
Entire sample	46,61	50,00	0,00	100,00

Table 11.2 Approximately what percentage of your culled book collection is given away to schools, libraries, charitable agencies or other venues? Broken out by Population of Library Service Area

Population of Library Service Area	Mean	Median	Minimum	Maximum
Less than 3000	48,32	50,00	0,00	100,00
3000+ -7000	33,92	15,00	0,00	100,00
7000-19000	46,17	50,00	0,00	100,00
More than 19000	56,14	65,00	2,00	100,00

Table 11.3 Approximately what percentage of your culled book collection is given away to schools, libraries, charitable agencies or other venues? Broken out by Size of full time equivalent library staff

Size of full time equivalent library staff	Mean	Median	Minimum	Maximum
1 or less	51,66	50,00	0,00	100,00
1+ -2.8	40,78	50,00	0,00	85,00
2.8+ -6	43,00	40,00	0,00	100,00
More than 6	47,93	37,50	0,00	100,00

Table 11.4 Approximately what percentage of your culled book collection is given away to schools, libraries, charitable agencies or other venues? Broken out by Spending on print books ($)

Spending on print books ($)	Mean	Median	Minimum	Maximum
Less than 4500	52,35	50,00	0,50	100,00
4500-14000	42,21	37,50	0,00	100,00
14000-30000	49,58	57,50	1,00	100,00
More than 30000	42,85	20,00	0,00	100,00

Mention some incidents, if any, in which the library was forced to back track and restore access to print copies of materials that had been culled in printed form. Broken out by Population of Library Service Area

Less than 3000
1) n/a
2) We really cut down on our magazine subscriptions as people went to digital editions. Now we are seeing more patrons asking for print magazines again.
3) none
4) Worn-out classics have been added back in.
5) No comment.
6) movie and history related
7) No incidents
8) Books in Series
9) none
10) n/a
11) When the book was left on the shelf and patron has brought it up to check out.
12) N/A

3000+ -7000
1) n/a
2) Nancy Drew books - we pulled them as they weren't circulating and hadn't been and then sure enough girls started requesting them!
3) n/a
4) none
5) Books in a series
6) None
7) n/a
8) N/A
9) classics that became a movie hit
10) Those books that are part of a series.
11) n/a
12) none
13) N/A

7000-19000
1) n/a
2) This happens most often when series books are weeded.
3) none
4) n/a
5) The only instance where this might apply are materials that were pulled because of condition with the intention of repurchasing them.

6) n/a
7) none
8) None. Never happened (yet).
9) When the item appears on the Battle of the Books list, a book group chooses an older book and there are not enough copies in the system and/or sometimes a movie based on a book.
10) Interlibrary Loan
11) N/A

More than 19000

1) None.
2) No
3) None
4) Can't think of any
5) The library replaced about 20 books by different authors because they were pulled because of condition. The books were part of a series that are still popular.
6) None.
7) Mostly happens when something gets made into a movie and we have to reorder multiple copies.
8) None
9) Only in fiction where we no longer have a complete run of an author's works.
10) Most often someone will weed the last copy of a book that completes a set or series.
11) a couple of reference books
12) None.
13) Many people find it difficult to read a book on a tablet, e-reader, etc. on an ongoing basis. It bothers their eyes.

Support for Print or Digital

Are particular types of library users more likely to prefer print and lobby the library for more spending on print books?   If so who? Broken out by Population of Library Service Area

Less than 3000
1) my entire patronage
2) Nearly all. We've seen demand for e-books really drop.
3) adults like print
4) Older patrons prefer print.
5) Adult fiction readers
6) many people prefer printed books
7) No one lobbies for more books
8) Yes. That's against Federal Privacy Policy
9) I would say the elderly would be more likely to want a print book than an e-book. Usually they aren't the best candidates for change.
10) all
11) Most of our patronage prefers print, while there are some who have tablets or readers. Unfortunately we only have print collection at this time. We are working at acquiring an automation system. Maybe next year we will implement an eBook collection, if our budget allows.
12) Our Seniors still like a book in the hand.
13) Yes, the older population has the buying power and they prefer print.
14) The older patrons prefer print books especially large print.

3000+ -7000
1) The users who actually come to the library are the ones who prefer print. Digital users can access their materials without ever coming to the library.
2) No
3) n/a
4) Yes our senior citizens
5) Sure, those patrons who do not chose to read on electronic reading devices.
6) Longtime users. The new users are not aware that 95% of our collection isn't online. The problem is reaching them.
7) The majority of our library users have expressed the desire to maintain the print option.
8) Older patrons like print books. Younger patrons like eBooks.
9) yes- a lot of our users prefer print
10) Older people who do not want to learn how to use a tablet.
11) Younger
12) parents of young children
13) Yes. Senior Adults.

Public Library Plans for the Book Collection

7000-19000

1) no - but a lot of patrons like eBooks from WPLC
2) We have a large retirement community whose residents are not interested in learning skills needed to download books. Parents find a picture book more satisfying to hold and explore than an eReader or tablet.
3) no
4) older folks and mothers for their children
5) Older library users and parents of young children
6) The majority of our patrons. They are largely above 50, but many are tech savvy, however, they still prefer print. Or use both formats in different ways.
7) Older patrons who cannot use computers and digital devices. Patrons who cannot afford to have digital devices.
8) no
9) Older readers as a whole appear to prefer print books.
10) No. Many of our library users use both print and eBooks and for different purposes. I.e. they will load of their tablets before leaving on a vacation, rather than carrying books. They often have a book on one of their devices to read while waiting for something. The patrons who are most likely to use e-books over print books from the library; mostly did not use the library for book checkouts. . They already purchased their own copies. However, we do not see a dramatic drop in the number of donated books.
11) No
12) Patrons will tell us in conversation that they prefer print. The patrons are young, senior and teens. I think that some young people might have a preference for the eBook but they also are often not library patrons.
13) A large percentage of our patrons are 65+ and prefer print vs. digital content.
14) Seniors Parents of young children

More than 19000

1) Over 50 and parents of young children.
2) Yes, our older patrons and Friends of the Library.
3) Not that I know of.
4) No
5) My older patrons ask for more large print, I have several patrons who lobby for audio books. The audio books have been supplied through a shared database as have eBooks.
6) No one so far.
7) Senior citizens and families with young children.
8) Seniors
9) Avid readers read both eformat and print. The rest don't care enough to lobby for more spending print.
10) We find that, while most of our users still prefer print, the ones who bemoan the loss of print tend to be the ones who rarely use the library. Our power users have embraced digital.
11) older patrons aged 50 and older
12) Many older readers do not want to buy eReaders.
13) Seniors, most people like to the feel of a book in their hands rather than an eBook,

14) No, the users are all ages, genders. Some prefer print, some prefer eBook. The usage reports from my eBook provider show .8% of cardholders are eBook users at my library.

How is print collection culling at your library organized? Which librarians are involved in the decision-making? Who makes the final decisions in particular areas? Who reviews decisions? Who overturns decisions? Broken out by Population of Library Service Area

Less than 3000

1) Librarian's choice as there is just one. I consult board if the cull is many of a particular genre or large in number.
2) Since we only have one employee, I am also the decision-maker regarding culling.
3) the librarian does all the decision making, it is done when there is time
4) This is a one-person operation. the board accepts my opinions totally
5) Library director makes the decisions. Her decisions are usually abided by.
6) Culling is done yearly after summer reading program ends. Library director and asst. library director work together to decide on which books to cull. Library director reviews and overturns decisions if necessary.
7) director
8) Board members cull as they have time
9) By looking at dates and shape of books. Library Director& Assistant Library Director, Gina Suson. No One. No One.
10) one person library
11) I make all the decisions, I have help from the 1 assistant that we have. I usually do a major weeding in the middle of winter. Then in spring we have a book sale.
12) The director has final say but it is a collaborative effort among the 3 of us.
13) There is only me. The board allows me to decide what to cull.
14) The ultimate decision rests with the library director.
15) I am the only employee I make all of the decisions

3000+ -7000

1) All culling decisions are made by the director. The director generates the reports and assigns staff to weed the items as needed.
2) We have a small library. Staff makes decisions but I make all the final decisions.
3) Acquisitions librarian and/or Library director
4) As needed. The Director in all instances
5) Director culls and makes the decision.
6) Librarian is in charge of these decisions.
7) Small library, 1 librarian, no problem.
8) Manager
9) Assistant librarians do the weeding and ask Director if they have a question. Director can overturn weeding decisions.
10) Library direction using data from our circulation system
11) Circulation staff look and age, condition, and circulation of a book, and suggest weeding. I review the suggestions and give the final say.

12) Me, only staff member. Occasionally have a volunteer to help.

13) Library manager makes final decision. Experienced staff work with library manager

14) Director and Assistant. Library Director.

7000-19000

1) Library Director makes the decisions - sometimes staff and volunteers make suggestions - basically up to director

2) Lists are made regularly of items that haven't circulated for three years. Circa aides pull the listed books. Anyone on staff can make an argument for keeping a book, but the director makes the final weeding decision.

3) full-time staff/manager

4) staff weeds

5) Adult and youth Librarians have control over purchase and removal of the items in their respective collections.

6) Library director makes the vast majority of all of the above decisions with input from staff where relevant.

7) Director and Head of the Children's Dept.

8) The head librarian is involved in the decision-making.

9) Since we are a small library, we generally cull as we have time, but no less than 2-3 times a year by sections. Not all of non-fiction is done at once. When certain areas in fiction become crowded, culling is initiated in that area. The library director (who is the book purchaser) is the person who decides what to cull.

10) The librarians responsible for ordering for an area are most likely to do the culling. That said. . We only have three people ordering (2 in children's) and myself the director for the rest of the collection. I have final say over all weeding decisions

11) Since, we are a staff of two, both the Library Director and the library assistant weed the collection, when needed.

12) At the local level the director would review decisions and overturn decisions if necessary. Our regional library system took responsibility for weeding the collection post flood.

13) Managers for each department choose materials as well as cull so that they are aware of what is needed to be updated, moved or added to. Director has final word on anything that is controversial or unsure.

More than 19000

1) Librarian/Director weeds main collection or provides training and guidance. Branch managers are trained to weed their collections.

2) We have a centralized collection development department. We have a media librarian, juvenile, and an adult librarian. I would say I as the collection development librarians make final decisions and I as the director have the ability to review and overturn them.

3) Each librarian at the branches is responsible for an area of the collection. Using our general guidelines they make the final decision about weeding an item. There is no formal review.

4) Director has final say but staff has a huge input, especially the ones who work out front as they know what's circulating and condition of items.

5) Department heads and staff members work together.

6) The library director decides where to weed. There is only one librarian in this library. It is a small rural library. The library board has the right to override decisions.

7) Director does it all.

8) We rotate through yearly and the technical services team does the majority of the organized weeding. The Circ-in team weed the damaged items as they come in.

9) Collection Development librarians make the decisions, and also review need to replace items in the collection. There is no decision review process.

10) We have 16 selectors who oversee the management of their areas of the collection. They make the final decisions. If a decision is overturned, it would be only because the selector was not getting rid of items that should not be in the collection. We see this as a training issue.

11) We have a three year schedule. The entire collection in all branches is weeded continuously using that schedule. All professional staff is involved, the branch manager has final decision authority in his/her branch. The two collection development coordinators can override branch managers

12) The collection developer and front line staff work together.

13) Librarians who purchase collections also weed them. Director reviews and may overturn.

14) All staff have the training and ability to cull materials. If some materials are questionable about being culled the Library Director makes the final decision

15) Youth Services Staff choose juvenile fiction and nonfiction books to be culled, the cart comes to Director for final.

What is the greatest mistake that the library has made in its print book collection development decision making in recent years? Broken out by Population of Library Service Area

Less than 3000
1) Little attention to middle school purchases.
2) Trying to please everyone. Libraries were pushed to really expand teen services and materials, and we expanded our Young Adult section and tried to get teen programming going with zero results. Try as we might, we just can't get most teens interested in anything but computer games. The teens who are in often and read voraciously are bypassing the YA books in favor of the adult section. The teen book offerings for several years were primarily dystopian or vampire books, and we've seen those circulation areas really drop off. Now we're stuck with a bunch of books that were supposedly popular, but never circulated and are now being culled in like-new condition, but nobody wants them, schools included, as they are dealing with the same issue.
3) the former librarian weeded too many books
4) Purchasing one-shot authors, when the work was not well-reviewed to begin with.
5) No comment.
6) getting rid of a printed books later requested
7) No mistakes
8) Order a book that we already have.
9) don't know of any, no one has complained as we can order any book from other libraries
10) A couple of Biographies, and a couple of westerns.
11) Previous librarian was adding books to the collection that was not paid for.
12) Junior biography.
13) Nothing comes to mind.

3000+ -7000
1) not sure
2) See Nancy Drew above!
3) n/a
4) needing more funds
5) Probably ordering more than one copy of a publication. Our shelf space does not permit several copies of a particular read.
6) Duplicate purchasing because of publishers changing titles in reprints of old historical works.
7) Purchasing Best Sellers
8) N/A
9) Letting bestselling list dictate what we purchase
10) Buying books "just in case someone may want to read it."
11) Not moving to eBooks sooner.
12) We don't make mistakes, unless it is buying books by Glen Beck!
13) N/A

Public Library Plans for the Book Collection

7000-19000

1) can't think of anything
2) not keeping up with the changes in young adult fiction
3) not setting weeding goals
4) In a funding crisis, the previous administration added all donated materials to the collection to provide "new" items regardless of content or redundancy. We have spent the last 4 years removing the majority of these and the other superfluous items that should have been removed long ago.
5) We are struggling with determining which YA books appeal.
6) not buying duplicate copies of popular books
7) Not having a more consistent budget for each area of our collection.
8) Selecting juvenile books simply because they won awards (Caldecott and Newbery, in particular) many many years ago. They are no longer very attractive and have received little attention from browsers and readers.
9) According to our statistics, I'm comfortable with our collection development decisions. Always I can find individual titles that just never appealed to our patrons, but they are infrequent.
10) No, mistakes. We utilize the proper tools to weed the collection.
11) We are very comfortable with the decisions made prior to the flood, however, space was becoming an issue. The flood forced deep weeding that may well have been necessary.
12) culling without discrimination

More than 19000

1) Forgetting to look at the size of the book. We do not have space for oversized coffee-table type books. We make few mistakes as we are in tune to patrons existing needs and anticipate their future informational needs.
2) Two years ago, we misread reports in CHQ and weeded too aggressively. We have been making up for that ever since.
3) Maybe too many non-holdable copies. We have served our browsing patrons very well, but I think we need to meet the needs of our patrons who only place holds. Those are the Amazon shoppers. Let's try to nail that market.
4) Not being able to keep print materials in some areas up to date due to budget.
5) Can't think of any.
6) We have not been able to fund a broader range of material in Large Print. Westerns circulate the best, with Best Sellers second. The cost of large print prohibits us from a broader depth of material.
7) Not a mistake, just a change... about 5 years ago Large Print use had increased so we increased the purchasing of large print titles. Then 3 years ago, it plummeted...those readers have almost all gone to eBooks.
8) Getting too technical in adult non-fiction titles. Those titles just don't circulate.
9) Not switching to eBooks sooner.
10) None
11) The most controversial decision was to not add 50 Shades of Gray to the collection.
12) Hmmmm.......cannot think of a greatest mistake.
13) Can't think of any
14) Adding to YA nonfiction. There is little to no usage even on new items.

What advice do you have for your peers on planning for the future in public library book purchasing? Broken out by Population of Library Service Area

Less than 3000
1) none
2) Don't abandon print books in favor of the latest fad. We're so glad we proceeded cautiously with digital books as we've seen demand remain strong or increase for print books over e-books.
3) Research all options, thrift stores, used books, amazon etc.
4) Read reviews - lots of them. Make your dollars count for the best of the best. Pay attention to what your readers want, and then try to meet some of their requests.
5) No comment.
6) listen to the patrons wants and needs
7) Have a budget allotment for book purchasing
8) Pay attention & take your time when ordering.
9) depend on your patrons to know what they read
10) Hold onto your budget! If you can't get it increased, do all you can to ensure it isn't decreased. The public is rarely well informed about how a library is funded. Make sure that your community understands where your funding comes from, how it compares to other similar sized libraries, and what all that funding pays for, and the future of that budget. If we don't educate them to the hardships of budgeting a library, they will never know the struggles we go through just to keep our doors open.
11) Listen & watch what your patrons are checking out & their interest.
12) Know your patrons wants.
13) Know what your patrons are interested in.

3000+ -7000
1) Classics are classics for a reason - even books such as Nancy Drew, Hardy Boys, etc. Be careful about weeding those!
2) I am an advocate of eBooks, but not as a primary reading source. There has been too much (scientific) information just within the last year on the benefits of print books versus eBooks. I think eBooks should be an addendum to a print collection. I also believe any library has to tailor their collection for the patrons in the area they service.
3) get more funding
4) Read, read, read the reviews of the books, meet the authors, if possible,(especially those in your area); go to conventions; enroll in webinars; visit with neighboring librarians and most importantly know your readers and interest groups in your service area.
5) In the local history/genealogy area, publishing is easy now, and often small quantities or print-on-demand. Therefore no publisher is advertising for the author, and librarians have to work hard to even know that something new is in print.
6) Look outside the box and not just the best seller lists there are many wonderful authors who are not best sellers but are enjoyable.
7) Know your patrons and what they are interested in and looking for.

8) Go with the demand. Create your own demand

9) Be flexible.

10) ??

11) Take a deep breath and accept change

12) Possibly survey community.

7000-19000

1) Make sure that the items are relevant to your community

2) I would love to see consortia collection development. With the ease of ILL it makes sense that each library collects genres and subjects of local interest knowing that other libraries in the consortia will collect and retain other areas. Unfortunately, it appears that this sort of buying will be more difficult with eBooks than with print.

3) Be aware of your ILL requests

4) purchase for archival, not just best sellers list

5) Begin by evaluating your audience and space and plan accordingly

6) Know your patrons before making any significant decisions.

7) Invest in eBooks. We are small but we have garnered so many new patrons who go "ohhhhh, you do ebooks?"

8) Don't buy more multiple copies of a book than you really need to -- keep a close eye on it. We only purchase one copy for the most part because we are a small rural library, but multiple copies (even in eBooks) can be a waste of money that could go to a different title.

9) Know your patrons. Listen to your patron requests. Never assume you know 'what' is correct for your patrons. Balance the collection so that someone can walk out of the library with at least a start . . . Holds in a consortium are nice, but you want your patron to leave filling like he has a start.

10) Learn from your patron, what they like to read and purchase then. Even if it is on the NY bestseller list, it might not be what your patrons like to read. All libraries have patrons, who have different taste in reading choices. We listen to our patrons.

11) Pay close attention to what your patrons are indicating are their needs.

More than 19000

1) Do not purchase reference materials just because that is what has always been done. Make sure you are aware of your demographics and anticipate needs. A rural, small library will not have the scope of the collection of a larger library -- but, we provide access to all materials via ILL. Shelf-space is premium. If items are not being used, get rid of them.

2) Just realize that the world is constantly changing and you have to give your community not only what you want, but what they're ready for. Some communities may not be ready for so much online resources access.

3) Don't plan on eBook reading to take the place of print book reading. EBook readers read more of all formats. Make them all available. Downloadable audio is huge and it's only going to get bigger!

4) Listen to your users!

5) I think we are alive and well.

6) It is important to know your circulation, patrons, and to take chances on new authors. I read several blogs/Facebook pages for reviews by renowned reviewers. I also read reviews in Library Journal, Kirkus and Booklist. I talk with librarians around the state and participate in Good Reads advisory

with fellow librarians. Try to balance your purchases throughout the library with regard to age, interest, and needs.

7) Stay on top of *actual* usage, and be flexible and ready to change!

8) You need to have some "standard" titles but purchase what you know will circulate.

9) Don't wait - it only gets harder to catch up

10) Utilize a good tool such as Collection HQ. The data backs up decisions regarding removing items and assists in seeing more clearly what areas are heavily used.

11) Print books will be with us for a long time, but we don't need to feel threatened by the emergence of digital.

12) Know your community! Know where patrons get their books (in any form) if not you. Listen to your community and your board. Be creative. Don't think you can plan 5 years ahead; life changes.

13) Survey their users and non-users alike and follow their Plan of Service

14) I'm still learning myself. Don't be afraid to weed based on the CREW manual, you can't go wrong

Made in the USA
Middletown, DE
10 January 2016